Nothing About Baseball
Is Trivial

Nothing About Baseball Is Trivial

Essential Terms, Rules, Stats & History
for Fans and Wannabe Fans

First Edition

Dean Christensen

Published 2018

ISBN-13: 978-1727593631
ISBN-10: 1727593634

Printed in the United States of America by CreateSpace, Charleston, SC.

Front cover photo by Anneka. Used under license from Shutterstock.com.

Back cover photo by Henry Hazboun. Used under license from Shutterstock.com.

For Glenda, my MVP

(Most Valuable Person)

for over forty years.

Whoever wants to know the heart and mind of America had better learn baseball, the rules and realities of the game.

– Jacques Barzun

From *God's Country and Mine: A Declaration of Love Spiced with a Few Harsh Words,* (1954)

Introduction

In my earliest recollection of baseball, I am five years old, sitting on my older brother Ken's lap in front of the TV in the living room of our modest home in South Dakota. He was eighteen or nineteen and home from college for the summer. Our eyes were riveted to the action playing out on our seventeen-inch black-and-white television three feet in front of us. I didn't know a double from a double play or a walk from a warning track, but I knew that we were doing something special together: we were watching a baseball game. Ken did his best to explain what was happening on the field in terms a little tyke could grasp. I don't remember a word he said, but I remember the feeling. My big brother, whom I idolized, liked this thing called baseball—therefore I liked it. This was indeed Something Special. That very day the seeds were planted that grew into my own love of the national pastime.

Are you new to the world of baseball? Have you wondered what some of the peculiar words and phrases associated with the game are about? Are you hoping to make a good impression on a friend or loved one who loves the game? Do you wish you understood what the "national game" is all about, that you were better educated in the rules, trivia, and pleasures of America's greatest sport? This book is for you.

Or perhaps you are you a longtime, dyed-in-the-wool fan who enjoys watching, reading, and talking about your favorite sport, the national pastime. Perhaps you subscribe to MLB.com and watch as many games as humanly possible each season. You already know a lot about the game, but maybe there's something more—little tidbits of trivia to add to your enjoyment of the history of the game or aspects of baseball you were uncertain about. Then I thank you for holding in your hands this brief baseball lexicon, glossary, guidebook, or whatever you want to call it. I hope—and believe—that you will enjoy it.

I had started out to write a brochure-sized pamphlet with two or three dozen of the most common terms and expressions one might hear on a radio or TV baseball broadcast.[1] The intended reader was the person to whom the game and its terminology were mostly Greek, but who wanted to understand at least the basics when watching or listening to a game with a friend, spouse, or significant other who enjoys the game. I envisioned it as a simple resource to keep near the TV or radio (or computer) for handy reference.

As often happens with such projects, my little brochure took on a life of its own and grew into something larger. And while much of this book is aimed primarily at the wannabe fan, I believe that dedicated baseball buffs will find a surprising amount of interesting tidbits and juicy morsels among the more than 350 entries in the following pages.

Some would say this is nothing but trivial stuff. *Trivia* is the plural of the Latin *trivium*—"a place where three roads meet" (from *tri-* "three" + *via* "road"). The sense was that of a common, ordinary place where people crossed each other's paths and paused to shoot the breeze about everything and

---

[1] In retrospect a ridiculous objective.

nothing in particular. In time, those everyday topics of little importance or significance came to be known as trivia.[2]

I know people—friends of mine—who scoff at the idea of baseball (or any sport) having any real importance. I can allude to those people here because they obviously won't be reading this book! "It's just a game," they say, "and games are for play and leisure, not for serious living." To them, baseball is a mere dalliance, a distraction from important concerns. I see that point. Compared to the sometimes crushing burdens of sickness, poverty, pain, fear, dying, death, a crumbling relationship, family dysfunction, sin, and salvation—the real problems of life—baseball is a mere child's game; it is nothing. It is trivial.

And yet, as a sport, a pastime, and yes, a *game*, the importance of baseball resides in the mind of each beholder. Psychologist and philosopher Jordan B. Peterson, in a different context, writes of the importance of games: "Every game has rules. . . . You accept them merely by deciding to play the game. The first of these rules is that the game is important. If it wasn't important, you wouldn't be playing it. Playing a game defines it as important."[3]

Then again, sometimes as I reflect on my enjoyment of baseball I can identify with writer Roger Angell's candid confession: "I was suddenly taken by surprise—knocked flat, in fact—by a statistic that fell out of the sky, so to speak: I

---

[2] The *trivium* was also the designation for the so-called lower three of the seven subjects studied in classical education, namely grammar, logic, and rhetoric. They were supposedly the more common and therefore less important of the seven (the other four "higher" subjects being arithmetic, geometry, astronomy, and music).

[3] Jordan B. Peterson, *12 Rules for Life: An Antidote to Chaos* (Toronto: Random House Canada, 2017) 213.

have been a fan for fifty years. My first reaction, of course, was guilt. A half-century of vicariousness? Fifty years . . . In pursuit of a *game*? For shame sir!"[4]

Writer, political pundit, and baseball fan extraordinaire George Will observed, "Baseball, it is said, is only a game. True, and the Grand Canyon is only a hole in Arizona. Not all holes, or games, are created equal."[5] Baseball, like all sports, entertainments, and so-called distractions, can serve a purpose that is not trivial at all. Baseball gives us something neutral besides the weather to chat about for a minute with a neighbor on the way to the mailbox; it provides a common ground to share with fellow humans who are as different from us as banana cream pie is from pizza pie; it brings families and friends together at the ballpark or in front of the television to "root, root, root for [or against] the home team," and, as poet Joel Oppenheimer said, baseball "makes it easy for the generations to talk to one another." And if we can talk to one another, is that unimportant?

Baseball provides an escape from our worries for two or three hours to immerse ourselves in (dare I say it?) something *fun*. In our right minds we know that an indulgence in the wholesome fun of baseball won't solve all our problems. It

---

Correct thinkers think that "baseball trivia" is an oxymoron: nothing about baseball is trivial.

– George F. Will
(from his column of April 8, 1990)

---

4 Angell 1991, 117.
5 Will 1990, 294.

might not solve any of them. But don't we suspect that it could improve our outlook on life—our mental health—if only for a while. And doesn't that make a tiny contribution to the wholeness of our world? I think so.

Is baseball America's greatest sport? Sports fans go round and round on that, and I've heard all the arguments. Let them argue. I'm aware that, according to Gallup, football has been Americans' "favorite sport to watch" since the early 1960s. Today, four times as many Americans report that football is their favorite sport. In fact, baseball now ranks third, behind basketball and only slightly ahead of soccer.[6] Nevertheless, I'm also aware that in 2014 more than 35 percent of Americans said that they do follow baseball.[7]

My mind is made up: I'm unashamedly of the opinion that baseball is not only America's oldest and most truly "American" team sport but also our greatest sport. In my book (yes, this book, *and* the book of my heart—cue the violin music), baseball still deserves the moniker "America's National Pastime."

I write a blog called *The Dean's English*, which is all about language, grammar, vocabulary, and word usage. It's only natural for me to wed my love of language and words to my love of baseball and baseball history to create a brief baseball lexicon or glossary—a handbook that can easily be carried to the ballpark, reside comfortably next to your easy chair . . . or

---

[6] The Gallup poll, in December 2017, found that 37% of Americans say football is their favorite sport to watch or follow; basketball is second at 11%; baseball third at 9% (an all-time low, sadly); and soccer is fourth at 7% (Norman 2018).
[7] Source: www.statista.com/statistics/197882/us-adults-following-major-league-baseball-by-age/

occupy a prominent spot in the porcelain-throne "reading room."

Other books have been written with far more content, including the massive tome *The Dickson Baseball Dictionary*, a marvelous book that I recommend. But you'd have a hard time toting it to the ballpark or tucking it into your backpack. As much as I appreciate Dickson's book, I purposefully consulted it sparingly while writing this guide, to avoid the temptation to regurgitate an abbreviated version of it. I wanted the contents here to come mostly from my own experience as a lifelong baseball lover. However, I did consult Dickson and numerous other sources (see the bibliography in the back) for clarification or additional information on a topic when needed, because factual accuracy was a high priority. But for the most part, what you have here is the product of my lifetime enjoyment of the game and my broad baseball reading.

I've been an avid reader since childhood, and my lifelong appreciation of baseball has been deeply enriched over the years by reading a good deal of baseball history—all the way back to the earliest days of the game. I've drawn on that background to enhance this text by incorporating some illustrative material and examples from the sport's rich past. Along with that, I've interspersed a couple dozen of my favorite baseball-themed quotations throughout the text to provide humor and enlightenment where appropriate.

Sometimes self-doubt tried to derail me as I wrote. After all, who am I to produce yet another book on the wonderful game of baseball? I may be a lifelong dyed-in-the-wool fan and a writer, but I'm no "baseball expert." Then I ran across this quote from a true baseball expert if ever there was one, Bill James, telling of his wife's concern about not being an "expert" on baseball uniforms after contributing material on that subject for one of his books. James writes, "I've tried to tell her, as I've tried to explain to so many people, that when you write facts they are either true or they are false, and being an expert or not being an expert has absolutely nothing to do with it."[8] That made me feel better. (I'm easily consoled.) I have tried to write as factually and accurately as possible, carefully researching when in doubt or in need of additional material. I've also written of my own experience in a few places and included a few subjective observations and a handful of opinions here and there. You may agree or not agree at those points, and that's perfectly fine. But when factual content is involved, that is open to correction where error is made, and I invite you to let me know about it (my email address is on the copyright page).

How to Use This Book: Five Important Points

1. This is a guidebook, a reference work. It is an A-to-Y collection of baseball-related topics that you can use like a glossary or a lexicon to look things up as needed or wanted. It's not necessarily my intention that you read it front to back, cover to cover. You can read it that way, of course, and if you do, I hope you'll find it informative and entertaining. You can read it any way you like. You can read it aloud, standing on your head on a park bench, if that's your thing.

2. Where another entry or topic from the book is referred to, it is formatted in SMALL CAPS. You will know you can read more about whatever that word or expression is under that entry in the book.

---

[8] James 1985, 5.

3. As to the use of masculine pronouns (*he, him, his*), let me say up front that I'm not a sexist, and I do know how to write gender-neutral content. But I'm also a realist. Unless otherwise indicated, the entries that follow pertain to the game of Major League Baseball (MLB) and the players of Major League Baseball. All MLB players in history, from its beginnings in the eighteenth century down to the present—all 19,360 of them—have been men. Have women played organized professional baseball in U.S. history? Yes, they have, and that fact is acknowledged within (see, for example, the entry on WOMEN'S PROFESSIONAL BASEBALL). However, Major League Baseball is and has been the domain of men, and so when pronouns appear, they will be masculine by default.

4. About the footnotes: I am a fan of footnotes if they enhance the reading experience. I prefer footnotes to endnotes because the reader doesn't have to waste time hunting in the back of the book for information that could be much more easily accessed right there at the bottom of the page. Are there too many footnotes? Probably. Nobody will force you to read them, but they're there for the nerds among us.

5. I followed the guidelines of the *Associated Press Stylebook and Briefing on Media Law 2017* for spelling, numbers, capitalization, and hyphenation for baseball-specific terms and statistics. I used the *Chicago Manual of Style* 17th edition for most other style questions.

I tried to include all the terms and expressions that one needs to know to understand and enjoy the game of baseball—and a lot more. Have I left any out that you think ought to be here? Probably. But I had to stop the ever-expanding list somewhere, or else the purpose of the book will have been defeated, which is to provide a *concise* handbook that can be easily carried around or that fits nicely beside the TV remote—or in the magazine basket next to the john. I admit, the latter location is a great place to thumb through these pages and read random entries, because the book doesn't have to be read like a novel or a biography.

So sit back and relax with some peanuts and crackerjack and enjoy the not-so-trivial game of baseball.

When you come to a fork in the road, take it.

– Attributed to Hall of Fame catcher Yogi Berra

Only boring people find baseball boring.

– Sportswriter Peter Golenboch

The Annotated Glossary

(See point 1 on page 7)

40–40 club – A reference to players who have hit 40 home runs and stolen 40 bases in the same season. It's an elite club—only four members in MLB history have done so: Jose Canseco, Oakland A's, 1988 (42 HR, 40 SB); Barry Bonds, SF Giants, 1996 (42–40); Alex Rodriguez, Seattle Mariners, 1998 (42–46); and Alfonso Soriano, Washington Nats, 2006 (46–41). Two other players have come within one HR of club membership: Bobby Bonds (Barry's dad), SF Giants, 1973 (39–43), and Matt Kemp, LA Dodgers, 2011 (39–40).

.500 ("five hundred") – The break-even winning percentage, when a team (or a pitcher) has won as many games as they have lost. It is the "percentage all professionals hope to attain at least, if not exceed."[9] It might also be a player's SLUGGING AVERAGE or similar statistic.

---

[9] Brosnan 1962, 25.

abbreviations – Baseball is loaded with abbreviations—shortened forms for its expansive range of statistics. Here are the most common ones you'll see:

1b	singles	hp	hit by pitch
2b	doubles	hr	home runs
3b	triples	ip	innings pitched
ab	at-bats	lhp	left-handed pitcher
avg	Average	lob	left on base
ba	batting average	pb	passed balls
bb	base on balls (walks)	pct	percentage
bfp	batters faced	po	putouts
bk	balks	r	runs
cg	complete games	rbi	runs batted in
cs	caught stealing	rhp	right-handed pitcher
dh	designated hitter (or doubleheader)	sb	stolen bases
dp	double plays	sf	sacrifice flies
er	earned runs	sh	sacrifice hits
era	earned run average	sho	shutouts
g	games	slg	slugging percentage
gf	games finished	so	strikeouts
gs	games started	sv	saves
h	hits	tc	total chances
hb	hit batters	wp	wild pitches

Abner Doubleday – Regarded as the "inventor of baseball" for much of the twentieth century, Abner Doubleday was a major in the Union Army during the Civil War. The legend, promoted by early baseball star and sporting goods magnate A.G. Spalding in the early twentieth century, was that Doubleday invented the game in 1839 in his hometown of Cooperstown, New York, while a cadet at West Point.[10] If this is what you've always heard and believed, I'm sorry to break it to you: historians years ago debunked the story as fictional; there's no virtually

---

[10] Which explains why Cooperstown was chosen for the home of the National Baseball Hall of Fame on its conception in 1935.

evidence that Doubleday ever saw or played, let alone "invented," baseball. Recently discovered newspaper reports prove that a version of "base ball" was played in Manhattan at least as far back as 1823, long before Doubleday supposedly invented the game.

ahead in the count – From the pitcher's point of view, when there are more strikes than balls in the COUNT. Theoretically, when ahead in the count the pitcher has the psychological advantage over the hitter, who may now be inclined to swing at a pitch out of the strike zone in order to STAY ALIVE, but which is more likely to result in his striking out instead. Conversely, when the pitcher falls BEHIND IN THE COUNT, the psychological advantage theoretically belongs to the batter.

air out – An out made by a fly ball, line drive, or pop-up that is caught by an infielder or outfielder.

alley, the – The expansive area in left-center field (between the left fielder and center fielder), or in right-center field (between the right fielder and center fielder). Sometimes the alley is referred to as THE GAP. A batter who hits a fair ball into the alley is more likely to reach base safely on a single or an EXTRA-BASE HIT.

All-Star Game (ASG) – Each year in July, Major League Baseball celebrates the finest players from both leagues in the All-Star Game. Purely an exhibition game that does not count in the standings, the first ASG was played at Comiskey Park, Chicago, on July 6, 1933, before more than 47,000 enthusiastic fans. Fittingly, "The Sultan of Swat," Babe Ruth, in the twilight of his illustrious career, slugged the first home run in ASG history, a two-run shot off Cardinals' left-hander Bill Hallahan in the third inning.

The AL won the game, 4-2. Since then, the ASG has been played every year except 1945, when it was cancelled due to World War II. Two All-Star games were played each year from 1959 to 1962. As of 2018, 89 All-Star games have been played, with the AL winning 44 and the NL 43, with two games ending in ties. The AL has won the last six straight games and 19 of the last 22. Perhaps proving the old adage that good pitching beats good hitting, in 32 games at least one team has scored one or fewer runs, and nine times the losing team has been shut out. Only six teams in All-Star history have scored runs in double digits—all six, interestingly, were AL teams—the last in 1998, when the AL beat the NL 13-8.

American League – One of two US major baseball leagues, consisting of 15 teams—five in each of three divisions: East, Central, and West. The American League (abbreviated AL) was founded in 1901, originally consisting of eight teams and no separate divisions. The league was administered by its own president and AL teams played NL teams only during the World Series each October (starting in 1903). Since 1997, with the inception of interleague play, AL teams play up to 18 regular-season games against NL teams. After the 1999 season, the AL and NL merged into a single organization presided over by a commissioner, and the league president became an honorary position. Since 2015, the honorary president of the AL has been Hall of Famer Frank Robinson.

around the horn – A double-play that begins with the third baseman fielding a grounder and throwing it to the second baseman for the first out, who throws it to the first baseman for the second out. Scored 5-4-3.

assist – An assist is credited to a fielder who throws a batted ball to another fielder that results in a PUTOUT. For example, a ground ball is hit to the third baseman, who throws across the diamond to the first baseman in time to put out the batter racing up the base line. The third baseman is credited with an assist on the play, and the first baseman is credited with a putout. If the throw is accurate and in time but the first baseman drops the ball so that the runner is safe, the third baseman is still credited with an assist, and the first baseman is charged with an ERROR.

at-bat – A player is credited with an official at-bat for a base hit, ground out, fly out, strikeout, or reaching base on a fielding error (including catcher's interference). No at-bat is credited for a base on balls, sacrifice hit, sacrifice fly, or being hit by a pitched ball.

attendance – The official paid attendance of every major league game is included at the bottom of the box score. Notice the word *paid* there. The paid attendance is not necessarily the same as the actual turnstile attendance. Teams count tickets sold (remember, professional baseball is about *money* to the owners)—including tickets sold that belong to season ticket holders, whether or not they are in attendance. Major League Baseball sells more tickets—and therefore records higher attendance figures—than any other professional sport in America by a huge margin. In 2017, although the average paid attendance at National Football League games was 67,405 and at Major League Baseball games it was 29,909, paid attendance at all MLB games was approximately 72.7 million, while total paid attendance at NFL games was about 17.3 million.[11]

If people don't want to come to the ballpark, how are you gonna stop them?

– Hall of Fame Catcher Yogi Berra

AVG (or BA) – Abbreviation for BATTING AVERAGE.

backstop – The high fence or screen located directly behind home base to protect spectators from foul balls. The official rules recommends that the backstop be located a minimum of 60 feet from home base.

BA (or AVG) – Abbreviation for BATTING AVERAGE.

bag – Another term for a BASE. Whereas home plate is rubber, flat, and level with the ground, first, second, and third bases are 15-inch square canvas bags, three to five inches thick, filled with soft material.

balk – An "illegal action" by a pitcher. When in the judgment of the umpire a pitcher in position[12] makes any motion which could potentially deceive the baserunner(s), the umpire will call "balk" and all baserunners advance one

---

[11] Attendance figures for MLB are from https://www.baseball-reference.com/leagues/MLB/2017-misc.shtml, and those for the NFL are from https://www.pro-football-reference.com/years/2017/attendance.htm.
[12] When a pitcher is "in position" it means he is standing on the pitcher's mound with his foot touching the pitcher's plate.

base. The official rule (6.02[a]) lists thirteen possible ways a pitcher can commit a balk.[13]

ball – There are two usages of *ball* in baseball: (1) the hard round white object with a cowhide cover held together with 216 red cotton stitches. It weighs just over five ounces and measures between 2.86 and 2.94 inches in diameter; (2) the home plate umpire calls "balls" and "strikes" thrown by the pitcher to the batter. A "ball" is a pitch thrown outside the strike zone—either inside or outside, or high or low—that the batter does not swing at.[14]

ball field – From the earliest days of baseball, the only space needed to play the game was a patch of ground big enough to accommodate a DIAMOND of some sort and an OUTFIELD. The arrangement was called a ball field, and boys and girls—but mostly boys in those early days—played on simple ball fields all over America. As the game developed and players formed organized leagues, ball fields gave way to BALLPARKs and STADIUMs.

---

[13] Just yesterday I was following an interleague game on the internet between the Dodgers and the Mariners. The score was tied 4-4 in the bottom of the ninth, and the home team Mariners were batting with one out; the bases were loaded. The Dodgers relief pitcher committed a balk and, as the broadcaster said, "Game over." The game-winning run scored from third. Not a pretty way to end a game, but I'm sure the Mariners will take it.
[14] A batter must either swing or not swing at every pitch thrown by the pitcher. If he does not swing he is said to be "taking" the pitch. If he takes a pitch out of the STRIKE ZONE—whether high, low, outside, or inside—the home plate umpire will (or should) call a ball. If he takes a pitch that is in the strike zone, the umpire will (or should) call a strike.

ballpark – A common term for the BALL FIELD and the structures surrounding it (i.e., the fences, seats, scoreboards, dugouts, bullpens, clubhouses, press boxes, etc.). Note that *ballpark* is ordinarily spelled as a closed compound.

[Baseball is] intimately wrapped up with one's youth. [It] is very much about being young again in a harmless way. That's why we call it a baseball park. You can call it a stadium if you want, but they were parks originally. "Park" is a Persian word and it means "paradise."

– Commissioner A. Bartlett Giamatti
(*Life* magazine interview, April 1988)

base – First, second, and third bases are 15 inches square and three to five inches thick, covered in white canvas, and filled with a soft material.

baseball, a (very) brief history of – Originally the word was written as an open compound (*base ball*), occasionally as a hyphenated compound (*base-ball*), and finally a closed compound (*baseball*). Contrary to a long-held popular myth, baseball was not invented by ABNER DOUBLEDAY in 1839 but evolved from the similar bat-and-ball games popular in England in the eighteenth century: cricket, rounders, and town ball. One New York newspaper account from 1823 tells of "active young men" in Manhattan playing the "manly and athletic game of base ball," which quickly caught on in popularity and became the "national game" played all over America.

It didn't take long for enterprising businessmen to look to the sport as a money-making endeavor. Hence, the Wright brothers[15] formed the first professional baseball team, the Cincinnati Red Stockings, in 1869. They went 57-0, but disbanded in 1870. The first professional league, the National Association of Professional Base Ball Players, was organized in 1871 and lasted until 1875. The National League of Professional Base Ball Clubs was formed in 1876 and has existed continuously since then. Today it is known simply as the National League. The American League was organized in 1901, and the two leagues have comprised what we now know as Major League Baseball ever since. Today 15 teams in each league play 162 regular-season games, followed in the post season by the Division Series in each league to determine the NL and AL champions, who finally meet each other in the Major League Baseball championship, the World Series, in October.

baseball: objectives of the game – Baseball "is a game between two teams of nine players each, under the direction of a manager, played on an enclosed field in accordance with these rules, under the jurisdiction of one or more umpires. . . . The objective of each team is to win by scoring more runs than the opponent."[16]

A regulation game consists of nine innings of three outs each; the visiting team bats in the top of each inning and the home team bats in the bottom of each inning. A game shortened due to inclement weather counts as official as long as a minimum of five innings have been played (or

---

[15] No, not *those* Wright brothers (Wilbur and Orville) but Harry and George Wright. Harry reportedly slugged 59 homers and batted over .500 during their 57-game schedule in 1869.
[16] *Official Baseball Rules 2017*, rules 1.01 and 1.05.

four and a half innings if the home team is leading after the top of the fifth).

baseball cards – The first baseball cards appeared in the 1880s, generally sold with cigars or cigarettes, and typically called "tobacco cards." Tobacco cards were very popular in the late nineteenth and early twentieth centuries. Men bought the tobacco and discarded the baseball cards, which boys retrieved and collected, playing with and trading them with their friends.

By the 1930s, tobacco cards had given way to bubblegum cards. As with tobacco, the purpose of the cards was to stimulate the sale of gum. In the mid-twentieth century, the Topps Chewing Gum company began marketing baseball cards directly to young boys by producing packs of cards that contained thin sticks of pink bubblegum. Topps standardized the size and basic design of the cards, which always included a portrait or action photo of the player on one side and biographical and statistical information about the player on the other. Baseball historian John Thorn writes, "[W]hat a marvel of compactness these cards were—the visage of a hero, the chronicle of his heroics, perhaps a tidbit of odd information or an amusing cartoon, a team logo, an autograph—and all on a piece of cardboard you could hold in your hand!"[17]

Other food and candy companies used baseball cards to sell their products. My first exposure, at the age of five in 1962, was through the Post company, which included eight or ten cards on the back of select cereal boxes. As soon as the Bran Flakes or Corn Flakes box was empty, I would cut out the

---

[17] Thorn 1998, 214.

cards as carefully as I could using my child-sized safety scissors. I still have five or six of those cards.

My first exposure to Topps was in 1964. That year they manufactured cards that were individually wrapped in green wax paper, with one stick of pink bubblegum, for one cent. In 1965, Topps sold five cards in a pack with one stick of bubblegum for a nickel. Adult men of my generation began to collect baseball cards in the 1980s and '90s, both out of a spirit of nostalgia and for an investment. By then I was able to do what I could never do as a kid: purchase an entire set of cards at one time.

As cool as that was, it just didn't quite compare to the excitement and mystery of buying cards a few at a time, unwrapping each pack, and thumbing through them in search of the star players, of which there were relatively few, compared to the many, many "common" players. Every baseball-card-loving kid had many copies of those "commons," which we used either for trade bait to get cards we didn't have, or to clip to the spokes of our bicycles to make them sound, kinda sorta, like motorcycles.

Today the nostalgia lives on for many of those adult collectors. Are cards a good investment? While many cards of the '50s, '60s, and '70s had appreciated in value greatly by the '80s, today, with the huge glut of cards flooding the market since then, baseball cards in general are not the sure-thing investment collectors hoped they would be. But boys (and girls) still enjoy them.

Oh, one more thing: I was a weird kid who played baseball games with my Topps cards, using my bed for the playing field and a small pencil eraser or a button for the ball. I still remember the thrill of those towering homers smacked by my Harmon Killebrew card over the headboard. I thought I was the only person on earth who did this, until years later I learned that a colleague of mine at the university did the exact same thing with his cards on his bed when he was a kid. Ah, baseball! (Ah, nerds!)

For many, baseball cards are the last toy as well as the first possession. You fall in love with them as a child, then leave them behind at puberty. They line the blue-water, lazy-day joy of childhood summers with the pride of blossoming maturity.

– Writer Thomas Boswell

---

base hit – The term for any batted ball that falls into fair territory in which the batter reaches first base (single), second base (double), third base (triple), or home plate (home run)—although most commonly a SINGLE is what is meant by "base hit." (A batted ball that is not handled cleanly by a fielder, in which the batter reaches base, is not a base hit. It is an error.)

Pete Rose holds the all-time record for base hits with 4,256. Ty Cobb is second all time with 4,191. They are the only two major leaguers with over 4,000 hits.

baselines (or base lines) – The white lines, marked usually with paint or chalk, that extend from home plate to first base and from home to third base. The lines continue beyond the bases as FOUL LINES all the way to the outfield fence.

base on balls (walk) – A batter is awarded first base when he takes four balls—balls pitched out of the strike zone that he does not swing at—during an at-bat. (Plural is *bases on balls*.) The more informal (and more common) term is *walk*, which is used both as a verb and a noun. ("Gonzalez walked two batters in seven innings today. He's now given up 35 walks on the season.")

baserunner – A batter who has reached first, second, or third base safely and either scores a run, is put out on the base paths, or remains on base until the inning is over.

bases loaded – The bases are "loaded" when runners simultaneously occupy first, second, and third bases with two or fewer outs.

bat – One of three essential pieces of equipment needed to play baseball. You've got to have a ball, you've got to have bases—even reasonable facsimiles of bases will do, such as pieces of cardboard, big rocks, pie tins, or bare patches of dirt—and you've got to have a bat. You don't have to have a glove to play baseball. It certainly helps, of course, but in the early days of the game, no one had gloves—at least nothing like modern gloves. You can play baseball without a glove, without a facemask, without a cap, or a helmet, or cleats. But you can't play baseball without some kind of a bat. The official rules specify that the bat "shall be a smooth, round stick not more than 2.61 inches in diameter at the thickest part and not more than 42 inches in length. The bat shall be one piece of solid wood" (Rule 3.02a).

The majority of bats used in major league baseball—all of them made of wood—are manufactured by the Louisville

Slugger® company in Louisville, Kentucky. For decades, almost all bats used by big leaguers were made of ash, weighed between 36 and 38 ounces, and measured around 35 inches in length. In recent years, more and more players use lighter bats (31 or 32 ounces) made of harder wood (maple or birch) that have more torque, which is one factor in the significant increase in home runs in the past 20-25 years.[18]

batter – On any given pitch, a batter has basically three options: swing away, take, or square around (to bunt). The batter will normally make the decision himself to either swing away or take based on his quick assessment of the pitch, whether it's in the strike zone or not.

The manager will decide if he wants the batter to lay down a BUNT, either for the purpose of sacrificing himself and making an out to move up the base runner(s) or to try to reach base successfully on a bunt single. The latter is normally is a tactic reserved for batters who are both skilled bunters and fleet of foot.

batter's box – A batter's box is positioned on either side of home plate, the one of the left side (facing the pitcher's mound) is for right-handed batters; the one on the right side is for left-handed batters. The batter's box is a rectangle six feet long by four feet wide. Once a pitcher comes to the SET POSITION or starts his WINDUP, a batter may not step out of the batter's box.

battery – The pitcher and the catcher together comprise a team's "battery." Although the first known use of the term was in 1868, baseball scholars are not of one mind on its

---

[18] Kiner and Peary 2004, 41; Siwoff 2018, 358-360.

origin. Two plausible explanations have been given for the term since the late 19th century: (1) it's an image borrowed from the world of electricity, in which the pitcher and catcher are like the positive and negative poles on an electric battery that powers the game—that generates the action; (2) it's an image borrowed from the military, in which a grouping of canon are called a battery, and soldiers loading the artillery fire lethal projectiles at an enemy. In baseball, the catcher provides the pitcher with ammunition after each pitch with which the pitcher loads in the artillery of his arm to fire away at the "enemy" batter. We may never know the exact origin, but the latter—the military analogy—makes most sense to me.

batting average – Abbreviated BA or AVG. The formula for calculating a player's batting average is simple: hits divided by at-bats. The range is .000 to 1.000. If a batter hits safely every time at bat, his batting average will be 1.000. No one in MLB history has batted 1.000 for a full season. Not even remotely close. Normally, a player is said to have a high batting average if it is above .300 (*three hundred*)—the game's standard of excellence. That's three base hits in every ten at bats. Typically, in recent years, the league batting champion will have a batting average between .325 and .360. The record for the lowest batting average ever to lead a league was set by Carl Yastrzemski of the Boston Red Sox in 1968, at .301. The highest average in the modern era (1920–present) was Rogers Hornsby's .424 in 1924.

To qualify for league leadership, a player needs 3.1 PLATE APPEARANCES (not at-bats) per team game played. Therefore, in a full 162-game season, a player needs 502 plate appearances to qualify for leadership in batting average (as well as slugging percentage, on-base percentage, and OPS).

bazooka – Slang for a pitcher's powerful arm.

beaning/bean ball – Term for a pitch or thrown ball that hits a batter—especially his "bean" (i.e., his head). One player in MLB history died from a beaning during a game. In 1920, the popular Cleveland Indians shortstop Ray Chapman was beaned in New York by Yankees pitcher Carl Mays. It's easy to imagine a white ball turning gray by the later innings, from dirt and spit, and then when the sun began to set in late afternoons—as it did on that fateful day in New York—it was often a challenge for batters to see pitches clearly. Eyewitnesses reported that Chapman never tried to get out of the way of the pitch that killed him, most likely because he never saw it.[19] Batting helmets were not introduced until the 1960s. Had they been available in 1920, its likely Chapman would have survived his beaning, at worst suffering only a mild concussion.

Star Boston Red Sox outfielder Tony Conigliaro had his all-star caliber career cut short by a beaning and resultant serious injury in August 1967, although he was able to play several more seasons before residual effects of the beaning forced him to hang up his glove for good.

behind in the count – From the pitcher's point of view, when there are more balls than strikes in the COUNT. Theoretically, the batter has the psychological advantage and the pitcher will more likely throw strikes, which an

---

[19] I became obsessed with the Chapman story 15 years ago, reading everything I could get my hands on about the incident, including the excellent book, *The Pitch That Killed*, by Mike Sowell.

alert batter can hit, which increases the probability of his reaching base safely. Conversely, when the pitcher is AHEAD IN THE COUNT, the psychological advantage (theoretically) belongs to the pitcher.

between the lines – Inside the regulation baseball field, where the fair-ball action takes place.

"Black Sox Scandal" – The moniker for the betting scandal of the 1919 World Series between the Chicago White Sox and the Cincinnati Reds. It was a best-of-nine-game Series that year that Cincinnati won 5 games to 3. An investigation afterward into allegations the White Sox had thrown the series for money found that eight Chicago players had colluded to fix the outcome in favor of Cincinnati. The first COMMISSIONER OF BASEBALL, Judge Kenesaw Mountain Landis, issued an order banning all eight players from major league baseball for life after the 1920 season. These eight included the legendary "Shoeless" Joe Jackson, an otherwise shoo-in to the Hall of Fame, whose lifetime batting average of .356 still ranks third highest in history. The great Ty Cobb, with the highest all-time batting average (.366), said that Shoeless Joe was the best natural hitter he'd ever seen. "Whenever I got the idea that I was a good hitter," he once said, "I'd stop and take a good look at [Shoeless Joe]. Then I knew I could stand some improvement."[20]

blocking the plate (by the catcher) – If a catcher is in possession of the ball, he may attempt to use his body to block home plate so a baserunner cannot easily score. A catcher who does not have possession of the ball may not block the direct pathway of a runner who is attempting to

---

[20] Leerhsen 2015, 383.

score. If so, the runner is safe. However, if the catcher blocks the pathway of a runner as the catcher is attempting to field a legitimate throw to the plate, there is no violation, and the normal rule for scoring a run (i.e., touching home plate) still applies.

blooper/bloop single – A soft line-drive that falls into the shallow outfield just beyond the reach of infielders or outfielders.

blown call (by the umpire) – Major league umpires are, on the whole, astoundingly skilled in their craft. But they are human, and every now and then an umpire will make a call that every spectator and their uncle knows is wrong—usually because we can see the replay in slow motion from five different camera angles. When that occurs, the error is informally known as a "blown call."

blown save – A relief pitcher who enters a game in a SAVE SITUATION and does not hold the lead until the completion of the game—and so fails to earn the save—is credited with a blown save.

blowout – (n.) A one-sided game in which one team outscores the other by a large margin.

board games (baseball) – I debated whether I should include something about baseball board games—it seems a  bit off topic. But it's meaningful to me—as it might also be to other baseball nerds—so here it is.

I don't remember how I acquired my first baseball board game, but I do remember how old I was (ten) and where I lived (Loveland, Colorado). The playing field, the cool artwork, and the standup scoreboard fired my imagination.

I'd never been to a real-life big league game, but in my mind, I was there. I played the game dozens of times—sometimes with friends, sometimes by myself. An older cousin who played it with me one afternoon in that summer of 1967 taught me how to keep score, and I have used his system, with only minor modifications, ever after.

Today that well-loved and oft-played board game is sitting on a shelf in my closet at home, more than fifty years later. Little did I know then that that Parker Brothers' game would be only the first of many I would own through the years. It was the catalyst that ignited the fire of my love affair with baseball board games.

I have owned (and played) many others, all of which—besides the Parker Brothers game—were "statistics-based" games, in which players were rated individually for hitting and pitching according to their actual performance in a particular season. Many of these game companies updated their player cards or rosters each year with new ratings based on the stats of the previous season. Dice, spinners, or "fast-action cards" were used to generate random numbers and activate each play. These included Cadaco's All-Star Baseball (only hitting was rated; pitching was a nonfactor), Negamco's Major League Baseball, Gil Hodges' Pennant Fever, Statis Pro Baseball, Pursue the Pennant Baseball, Strat-O-Matic® Baseball, APBA® (pronounced *ap-bah*) Pro Baseball, and Dynasty League Baseball. The Pursue the Pennant and Dynasty League games were by far the most

realistic in terms of batters' and pitchers' ratings, ballpark effects, play variability, although Strat-O-Matic, APBA, and Statis Pro weren't far behind in realism. All five of those generated pretty realistic stats. Most of these board games can be played either with a friend or solitaire in 30-45 minutes, which, for a nerdy, solitary kind of guy who loves baseball, scorekeeping, and statistics, is a gaming experience made in heaven.[21]

bottom of the inning – Each inning of a baseball game has two halves: the top half—or the "top of the inning"—when the visiting team bats, and the bottom half—or the "bottom of the inning"—when the home team bats. The home team's last "ups" (or last at bats in the bottom of the ninth inning if they are tied or behind[22]) is an important aspect of the home team advantage, because if they score the go-ahead run, they win.

box score – Sportswriter Jim Murray said, "The baseball diagnosis is foolproof. The box score is the most reliable X-ray in the world."[23] Everything you need to know about the outcome of a baseball game is recorded in the box score, including the LINEUPS and the LINE SCORE, the winning and losing pitchers, a record of the hits, runs, home runs, RBIs, strikeouts, earned runs allowed, and numerous other important stats. It's all there—the ballgame in a nutshell. As a kid, the two things that caused me to first fall in love

---

[21] Several of these games are still being produced and updated annually, including Dynasty League, Strat-O-Matic, and APBA. Although Statis Pro went defunct nearly 30 years ago, a number of independent entrepreneurs continue to generate new player-card sets for the game annually and sell them on eBay.

[22] If the home team is ahead after the top of the ninth inning, there is no need to bat in the bottom of the ninth as they have won the game.

[23] Stewart 2007, 153.

with baseball (besides watching it on TV) were BASEBALL CARDS and the box scores in the daily newspaper. Today's box scores give far more information than they did when I was a kid in the 1960s.

The box scores in the daily newspapers were the only means baseball fans had for generations to find out how their favorite teams did in the previous day's (or week's) games. Box scores are not unique to baseball, but baseball was the first sport to publish them in newspapers over 160 years ago. Sportswriter Henry Chadwick, often dubbed the "Father of Baseball," has been credited with "inventing" the box score in 1859.

[A box score] is a precisely etched miniature of the sport itself, for baseball, in spite of it grassy spaciousness and apparent unpredictability, is the most intensely satisfyingly mathematical of all our outdoor sports.

Roger Angell, *Once More Around the Park* (1991)

---

brush-back pitch – An intentional pitch high and inside that forces the batter to lean back away from home plate. The purpose of the brush-back is to keep the batter on his heels and off balance, thus reducing the likelihood that he can extend his arms, lean into the pitch, and make solid contact with the ball. While not thrown often, when it is used it is typically against a team's better hitters and sluggers—perhaps with a batter who belted a home run in his previous at bat. Sometimes, of course, the ball gets away from the pitcher and hits the batter, in which case he immediately takes his base (if no brawl ensues, which does happen on occasion).

buff – A devotee or follower of baseball—as in "My son is a huge baseball buff." The term originated in New York City in the early twentieth century, when boys and young men would gather to cheer on firefighters, who wore buff leather coats while battling conflagrations. Soon, the young spectators themselves came to be called "buffs," and eventually the word was used for fans of all sorts of things[24]—like baseball, of course. Further examples include car buff, film buff, word buff, English buff, classical music buff, classic rock 'n' roll buff, and running around in the buff buff.

Of course, there is also the well-loved (and more common) term FAN and the older monikers, "BUG" and "CRANK."

bug – A term for a baseball fan, popular between roughly 1904 and 1916. Its origin probably came from the idea of being bitten by a "bug" (or germ or virus) and getting sick with a fever. We still use the term today ("He came down with some sort of bug and was sick for a week"). In the early twentieth century, a baseball devotee might say he was stricken with baseball fever—that he had "caught the baseball bug." It didn't take long for the "sickness" to be applied to the person him- or herself: one didn't simply *catch* the bug, one *was* a bug—a baseball bug. The term caught on for a while, made popular by several Tin Pan Alley songs. By 1920, the term FAN, which antedates *bug* in baseball legend and lore, regained its dominant place in the American sports lexicon.

---

[24] Forsyth 2011, 74-75.

But I'm a fan of the archaic, the quirky, and the different. So frequently, I'll describe myself as a baseball *bug*.

Deal with it.

"Bug" as thus applied I find means a person of peculiar eccentricities, born of frenzy and expressed in wild, incoherent shrieks that develop a monomania called baseballitis.

– Actress Lillian Russell, quoted in "Rejuvenation of a Fan," *Baseball Magazine*, 1909.

---

bullpen – A designated space on the field, outside of fair territory, where relief pitchers sit during the game and where they warm up their arms before coming in to pitch. Each team has its own bullpen, which is usually located behind either the left field or right field fence. In some instances, where a stadium has a particularly large foul area, the bullpen may be located outside the left and right field foul lines, unprotected from the action on the field.

The term bullpen is also used figuratively for the group of relief pitchers themselves. A broadcaster might say that a team's "bullpen has been rock solid this season" or that "the bullpen has been overworked the past five games and is desperately in need of rest."

bunt – There are two methods of hitting (or attempting to hit) a baseball with a bat: swinging and bunting. To bunt, the batter simultaneously crouches, pivots so that he's facing the pitcher with his body, and moves his top hand up the barrel of his bat several inches. The object is to allow the bat to meet the ball softly—to "push" the ball—so that it rolls only a few feet from the batter's box toward first base or third base. The bunt is typically used when there is at least one runner on base and less than two outs, usually to make a SACRIFICE HIT in order to advance the baserunner(s). Most bunts are attempted by pitchers because they are typically the weakest hitters on the team;[25] if they can at least advance the baserunner(s)— even by sacrificing themselves—they will contribute more to their team's offensive efforts than if they did what most pitchers do most of the time: strike out. Occasionally, a speedy non-pitcher—usually a left-handed batter—will surprise the defense by attempting to lay down a DRAG BUNT for a base hit.

Fun fact: originally, bunts were called "baby hits."

bush league – A minor league. Sometimes a disparaging term for a player's or team's substandard play: "They're playing bush league ball this season."

called strike – There are two types of strikes: a swinging strike (which includes swings-and-misses and a foul balls) and a nonswinging strike. When a batter takes a pitch in the STRIKE ZONE, the umpire will call it a strike. Occasionally, a batter will TAKE A PITCH that isn't in the strike zone, and the umpire misjudges it and calls a strike. Nonetheless, if that's what the umpire calls it, that's what it is. Arguing balls and strikes will get the player (or manager, pitcher, catcher, whomever) thrown out of the game.

---

[25] Of course, we're talking about National League pitchers mainly as it is the league in which pitchers still bat.

can of corn – A nickname for a high, arcing FLY BALL. It originated in the late nineteenth century when grocers would stack canned fruits and vegetables on high shelves and use a hooked stick to pull a can from the top of the stack and catch it like an outfielder snagging a fly ball.[26] Why a "can of corn" instead of a "can of beans" or "can of apricots"? Probably because the alliterative expression just sounded better: "Jones hits a can-o'-corn to center field. DiMaggio is under it and pulls it in."

catch (play catch, have a catch) – When two or more players throw a ball back and forth in order to warm up or to practice fielding skills. The expression "have a catch" occurs in the classic film *Field of Dreams*, an expression almost no one I know ever heard of apart from the movie. I kind of like it, though.

catcher – The player on defense who plays behind home plate and receives the pitches. He calls for certain pitches—such as a curve low and outside or a fastball high and inside—using hand signals or "signs." He sometimes signals the fielders where to position themselves for certain batters. Occasionally, the catcher will look toward the dugout to the manager for instructions and then convey the manager's wishes to his pitcher or teammates. The catcher needs to study the hitters, know his pitchers, and understand the game of baseball as well as or better than his teammates. He needs to be strong and courageous, with a keen eye and a quick, accurate throwing arm.

catcher's interference – In the nineteenth century, when often only one umpire officiated ballgames, it was fairly

---

[26] Pinker 2011, 149

common for catchers to physically interfere with hitters while they stood in the batter's box, like tipping their bats when they were about to swing at a pitch. Thus the origin of what exists now as rule 6.01(c), which specifies that a batter be awarded first base if a catcher (or any fielder) physically interferes with him while batting. Today, while rare, such interference does occur occasionally.

caught napping – When a runner is standing off his base between pitches and is picked off by a quick throw by the pitcher or catcher, he is said to be "caught napping."

championship games/season – The technical term for games played during the regular season, which count in the standings, as opposed to exhibition games such as spring training games or the All-Star Game, which do not count in the standings. Since 1962, the championship season has been 162 games long for all major league teams. Prior to that, all the way back to the turn of the twentieth century, the season consisted of 154 games.

changeup – See TYPES OF PITCHES.

checked swing – A batter who begins to swing at a pitch but holds up before his bat crosses home plate has checked his swing. It is a judgment call by the umpire as to whether the batter checked his swing or not.

chin music – A ball pitched high and inside, near a batter's jaw. When thrown intentionally—sometimes to force a batter not to crowd the plate—it is often called a "knock-down" or "brush-back" pitch.

choke up – To move the hands up the barrel of the bat (away from the nob) anywhere from an inch to a few inches. Choking up gives the batter a slightly less powerful but slightly quicker, more controlled swing. Although seen much less frequently in the home run-happy 2010s, the technique is used by some batters in a two-strike situation to help them simply meet the ball and put it into play.

circus catch – A difficult and dramatic catch made (usually) by an outfielder, after sprinting some distance after a fly ball and leaping or diving to make the catch.

cleanup hitter – If the first three batters in the lineup reach base, thus loading the bases, the fourth batter can potentially "clean up" the base paths with one swing by hitting a home run. Thus, the fourth batter up, who typically is one of the team's better sluggers—if not the heaviest hitter on the block—is traditionally called the "cleanup hitter."

closer – The informal title of the relief pitcher who is called upon at the end of a game, usually during a SAVE SITUATION. Most teams have at least one pitcher—often a power pitcher—whose main role is to shut down the offense, to "close the door" on opposing hitters, thus ensuring his team's victory and earning the SAVE.

coach – Not to be confused with the manager. Coaches are subordinate to and assist the manager with various aspects of skills training, and they serve as in-game advisers for both players and the manager. Most teams have a pitching coach, hitting coach, first base coach, third base coach, bench coach, and a bullpen coach. During the game, while the team is up to bat, the base coaches stand in long, rectangular "boxes" marked on the field outside the first and third base foul lines; their job is to coach hitters and baserunners with hand signals and verbal instructions.

Arlie Latham of the Cincinnati Reds was the first full-time major league coach, in 1900.

clubhouse – The room or rooms underneath the stadium that contain a team's lockers, showers, offices, meeting areas, and so forth. Each team has its own clubhouse where players suit up before the game and to where they return after the game to shower, eat, debrief, and talk to the press.

Commissioner of Baseball – A scandal rocked the world of major league baseball following the 1919 season, when it was alleged that eight members of the Chicago White Sox had colluded to fix the World Series that October.[27] Baseball's owners decided that a central authority was needed to deal with that crisis and to restore a sense of integrity to a sport that had become increasingly corrupt. A federal court judge with a reputation for toughness, Kenesaw Mountain Landis,[28] was appointed as the first commissioner in 1920. In his role, Landis was granted almost unlimited ruling authority over major- and minor-league baseball. One of his first official acts was to ban for life the eight players accused in the aforementioned scandal, including Shoeless Joe Jackson, one of the greatest hitters of all time. Judge Landis served as commissioner for 24 years until his death in 1944 and did much to restore baseball's credibility in the eyes of the public.

A.B. "Happy" Chandler succeeded Landis as the second commissioner, and following Chandler, eight more men have served in the role now recognized as MLB's chief

---

[27] Often dubbed the "BLACK SOX SCANDAL."
[28] For those who may be wondering—there is only one *n* in Judge Landis's first name (unlike the Civil War battle site for which he was named).

executive officer. One of these was A. Bartlett Giamatti, former president of Yale University and scholar of medieval and comparative literature, who in 1989 suspended all-time hits leader Pete Rose from the game for life for his alleged betting on baseball. In 2014, Rob Manfred, a 56-year-old one-time labor relations lawyer from New York, was elected as the game's tenth (and current) commissioner.

The commissioner is elected to a three-year term by team owners.

complete game – A pitcher who starts and finishes a game has pitched a "complete game." Typically, this means a nine-inning game, but that number can vary because of various factors, e.g., a rain-shortened game, an extra-inning game, or a game pitched by a visiting pitcher in which the home team was ahead after the visiting team batted in the top of the ninth. (The home team would not bat in the bottom of the ninth.) In the last thirty or forty years, the role of relief pitchers has become more and more dominant, and therefore starters have been pitching fewer and fewer complete games. For example, in the 2017 season two AL pitchers tied for the major league lead in complete games: Corey Kluber of Cleveland and Ervin Santana of Minnesota each had 5. By contrast, in 1986, Fernando Valenzuela of the Dodgers led the majors with 20. In the 1960s and '70s, top pitchers routinely had 25–30 complete games.

The records in the MODERN ERA for most complete games pitched in each league are 650 by the American League, in 1974, and 546 by the National League, in 1971. The all-time records for *fewest* games pitched in each league were both established in 2017, with 32 by the AL and 27 by the NL.

That's an average of just 2 complete games per *team* for the entire season.

What's the all-time record for most complete games by an individual pitcher? In 1879, the Cincinnati Reds of the fledgling National League played 81 games. Right-hander Will White started 76 of those games and completed 75 of them.[29] The record in the Modern Era is 36, by Bob Feller of the Cleveland Indians, in 1946.

contact hitter – A hitter with good bat control who excels in hitting ground balls and line drives—especially to the right side—to advance baserunners, stay out of the double play, and keep from striking out.

corner – There is more than one "corner" in baseball. The area in left field and right field where the foul line meets the fence is called the corner. Sometimes the left and right fielders are called "corner players." A fair ball hit into the corner that is not caught by the outfielder usually results in an EXTRA-BASE HIT. Then there are corners in the diamond itself, at first base and third base, the latter often termed the "hot corner." When the defensive team is anticipating a bunt from the batter, the first and third basemen will often play "in" (i.e., closer to home plate than usual). It is said they are playing "in at the corners." Finally, "corners" is used to describe the outside and inside portions of the strike zone (i.e., over home plate), and a skilled pitcher is likely to achieve success if he consistently "paints the corners."

---

[29] Of course, the game was quite different in those early days; pitchers did not throw nearly as hard, for one thing, and many pitched underhand.

count – The running total of a batter's balls and strikes during an at-bat. Balls are always cited first and strikes second, and the home plate umpire keeps track. For example, a count of 2 and 1 (or 2–1) is two balls and one strike. A pitcher is said to be ahead in the count when the batter has more strikes than balls. For example, a pitcher is ahead in counts of 0–1, 0–2, and 1–2. Conversely, a pitcher is "behind in the count" when the batter has more balls than strikes (i.e., counts of 1–0, 2–0, 3–0, 2–1, 3–1, and 3–2). A "full count" is 3 balls and two strikes (or 3–2). Often, when the count is full and there are runners on base with two outs, the runners will break for the next base as soon as the ball leaves the pitcher's hand.

crank – When the United States began to recover from the terrible trauma of the Civil War in the 1860s, '70s, and '80s, baseball provided a healing tonic for many Americans. As the game's popularity skyrocketed, newspapers featured detailed accounts of games, box scores reduced each contest to a quick-and-easy statistical snapshot, and top ball players—or "ballists"—became the idols of boys everywhere (men, too, if they were honest). Enthusiastic devotees rose up from all walks of life, but guardians of polite society frowned upon them and referred to them as "cranks," a pejorative term. A "crank," generally, was someone not right in the head—out-of-joint mentally, overly enthusiastic about a subject or activity. He was considered uncultured and unruly—not someone you'd want your daughter to socialize with at the church picnic.

The term remained in popular use until the early twentieth century, when BUG briefly vied with FAN for the most common designation, and *crank* gradually disappeared from everyday use.

cripple count – A count of at least two more balls than strikes: 3-0, 2-0, or 3-1.

cripple hitter – A hitter who tends to do very well against pitchers who are behind in the count.

curve/curveball – Also known as *the deuce, Uncle Charlie, bender, hook, yakker,* and other slang terms, some of which are not printable. For example, after Sandy Koufax struck out the great Mickey Mantle on a filthy curve in the 1963 World Series, Mantle reportedly said, "How the *** is anybody supposed to hit that ***?" A good curve is one of the most difficult pitches to hit. A physicist proved as long ago as 1959 that the ball actually does curve in flight and is not an optical illusion. According to legend, Candy Cummings discovered the curveball and first used it competitively in 1869. Some pitchers in history notorious for their wicked curveballs are Mordecai "Three Finger" Brown in the DEADBALL ERA, Sam "Toothpick" Jones in the 1950s, Camilo Pascual in the '50s and '60s, Koufax in the '60s, Bert Blyleven in the '70s and '80s, Dwight Gooden in the '80s and '90s, and Clayton Kershaw in the 2010s.[30] (See also TYPES OF PITCHES below.)

Cy Young Award – Given each season to the best pitcher of the American and National Leagues, as voted by the Baseball Writers Association of America. The award is named in honor of Denton True "Cy" Young, who pitched from 1890 to 1911 and won 511 games, by far the most in history—94 more than Walter Johnson, who was number two. It's safe to say it's an untouchable record. Cy Young

---

[30] Much of this material is from "Real Men Have Curves," by Tom Verducci, *Sports Illustrated,* May 29, 2017, 37-43.

was elected to baseball's HALL OF FAME in its second year, 1937.

The Cy Young Award was established in 1956; it was given to just one pitcher in the majors (not one from each league) for the first eleven years (1956-66). In 1967, Major League Baseball began selecting one pitcher from each league. Roger Clemens has received the most Cy Young awards (seven) and Randy Johnson is second all time (five).

daisy cutter – A sharply hit ground ball that does not hop, skip, or bounce. (Same as GRASS CUTTER or WORM BURNER.)

Delta Score (DS) – In playing with a large database of baseball statistics a few years back, trying to determine which stats were most closely statistically correlated with team winning percentages, I discovered that the OPS was the most strongly correlated offensive stat and the WHIP was the most closely correlated pitching stat. Then I divided the team OPS by the team WHIP (and multiplied it by 100, for the heck of it) and found the resulting statistic, a ratio of a team's offensive production to its pitching efficiency, to be even more closely correlated to winning percentage. I decided to name this new statistic the Delta Score, because Delta (Δ) is the Greek letter "D," and my first name begins with . . . well, you get the picture.

So the Delta statistically correlates positively more strongly with team winning percentage than any other statistic.[31] For example, in 2017 the team with the highest DS in the majors was Cleveland (at 67.9); they ranked second in MLB winning percentage. (The team with the second highest DS,

---

[31] For those familiar with statistics, in 2017, the Delta score for all major league teams correlated at .93, which is pretty darn close to a perfect correlation.

the Dodgers (at 66.8), had the highest winning percentage in baseball. The team with the lowest DS was San Francisco (at 49.6), and they ranked tied for dead last in winning percentage.

The Delta Score is one more way to evaluate a team's performance, explaining why they won or lost as many games as they did. It's simple, it's easy to calculate, and you'll forever thank me for telling you about it.

In case you missed it, here's the easy-peasy formula for the DS: 100*[team OPS/team WHIP].

designated for assignment (DFA) – A player designated for assignment is one who has been removed from his team's 40-man roster. Within seven days, he can be either traded or placed on "irrevocable waivers," which means his former team cannot withdraw the waiver request; if another team claims him, the first team receives no compensation.

designated hitter (DH) – In an effort to add more offensive punch to ball games, in 1973 the American League adopted the designated hitter rule. The DH—who is typically a slow-footed or mediocre-fielding SLUGGER—bats in place of the pitcher and does not play in the field. To this day in the major leagues, only the American League uses the DH. The National League has retained the traditional arrangement, which includes the pitcher in the batting lineup. In INTERLEAGUE PLAY, when games are played in American League ballparks (including during the regular season and the World Series), both NL and AL teams use the DH. When interleague games occur in NL parks, the DH is not used by either team.

diamond – Specifically, the diamond is the part of the playing field outlined by the base paths: home to first, to second, to third, back to home. The entire ball field is sometimes loosely referred to as the diamond.

Deadball Era – The so-called Deadball Era lasted from roughly 1900 to 1920 and was characterized by low-scoring games, few home runs, and lots of singles, doubles, triples, sacrifice hits, and stolen bases. Pitchers dominated the sport and typically pitched entire games. Often a team would play most of a game, if not the entire game, with one or two baseballs. When the ball went into the stands via foul or home run, fans were expected to give it back so it could be used over and over. As a result, a ball slowly turned to mush and simply didn't travel as far as a new ball did—it was "dead" by comparison.

Another factor that contributed to the "deadness" of baseball was the widening of home plate in 1900, from 12 to 17 inches, which provided a bigger target for pitchers. In addition, in 1901, it was ruled that a foul ball that wasn't caught was a strike (unless the batter had two strikes on him—as it is today). Taken together, these factors led to a substantial decrease in offensive production, lower batting averages, and fewer runs scored. The Deadball Era had arrived.

In the late 1910s, with the arrival of Babe Ruth, a pitcher who could wallop the ball over the fence more often than anyone ever before, the fans turned out in droves to see the spectacle. When team owners discovered how much money could be made by ensuring that more balls left the yard, they began to use new balls with a more tightly wound inner core—and they provided lots more of them, so that by the 1920s, fans could keep home run balls and foul balls.

The fresh new balls, in greater supply, ensured more and more runs and home runs. The "dead ball" era gave way to a "live ball era" in the 1920s, with Babe Ruth, Jimmie Fox, Rogers Hornsby and other sluggers leading the way. Fans turned out in greater numbers than ever before, reaffirming baseball as America's NATIONAL PASTIME.

dimensions of the playing field – The official rules specify that a major league ball field will have an infield that is 90-feet square (i.e., bases are 90 feet apart). It's been said that if the distance were 85 feet, fewer batters would be put out on ground balls to an infielder—especially on grounders hit to the left side of the diamond. If the distance were 95 feet, fewer batters would reach base safely on ground balls hit to an infielder, and virtually no one would be able to steal a base. Ninety feet was a stroke of genius.

The minimum distance from home plate down the foul line to the outfield fence must be 250 feet, although a minimum of 320 feet is preferred, and a minimum distance of 400 feet to center field is preferred. The pitcher's plate is to be 60 feet, 6 inches from home plate, and must be 10 inches higher than home plate. The distance across the diamond from home plate to second base, and from first base to third base, is to be 127 feet, $3^{3/8}$ inches. It is recommended that the distance from home base to the backstop and from the baselines to the nearest fence be a minimum of 60 feet.

Disabled List (DL) – A team may place an injured player on the DL in order to call up a player from their 40-man roster to take his place. DLs are of three official lengths: (1) the 7-day DL is strictly for a player who may have a concussion; (2) the 10-day DL—which is typically what is meant by the term "the DL"—is for players with any kind of injury or illness, and players must remain on the DL for at least 10 days.[32] He may remain on the 10-day DL for longer—even much longer—than 10 days, but the minimum is 10 days, and he still remains on the team's 40-man roster; (3) the 60-day DL is for more serious injuries or illnesses that may require a lengthy stint off the active roster. Moving a player from the 10-day DL to the 60-day DL removes the player from the 40-man roster so that his team can replace him with another player from their FARM SYSTEM.

DL – See DISABLED LIST.

double play – Where two outs are made with one batted ball. A typical double play scenario has a baserunner on first base when the batter hits a sharp grounder that is fielded cleanly by an infielder (most often the shortstop or second baseman, but sometimes the third or first baseman), who throws to the infielder covering second base to cut down the runner coming from first; he then pivots and throws to first in time to put out the batter running to first. Two outs for the price of one: a double play. There are several possible double play scenarios, the two most common are these:

> **the 4-6-3 double play** – the second baseman (POSITION 4) scoops up a ground ball and throws to the shortstop (position 6) covering second base for the first out, and then the shortstop throws to the first baseman (position 3) for the second out. The second baseman is credited with an ASSIST, the shortstop with a PUTOUT and an assist, and the first baseman with a putout.

---

[32] Older fans may remember the 15-day DL—and even older fans (like the author) may remember the 21-day DL. Those DLs no longer exist, having been replaced by the current 10-day DL.

the 6-4-3 double play – the shortstop (POSITION 6) scoops up a ground ball and throws to the second baseman (position 4) covering second base for the first out, and then the second baseman throws to the first baseman (position 3) for the second out. The shortstop is credited with an ASSIST, the second baseman with a PUTOUT and an assist, and the first baseman with a putout. The 6-4-3 double play is the most common combination in baseball.

drag bunt – A ball bunted by a speedy left-handed batter down the first base line, hit so slowly that the batter appears to be dragging the ball behind him for a few feet. It differs from the sacrifice bunt in that the purpose of the drag bunt is to reach base safely (a bunt single), whereas the sacrifice bunt is intended to result in an out at first base, for the purpose of advancing the baserunner(s).

dugout – Each team has its own bench for players to sit on during the game, which, according to the official rules (2.05), must be at least 25 feet from the base line, covered with a roof, and enclosed at the back and ends. This structure is called the dugout.

dying quail – a pop fly that drops suddenly and unexpectedly (perhaps because of a gust of wind) between fielders for a base hit.

earned run – In its most basic definition, an earned run is a run charged to a pitcher that is scored without the aid of an ERROR or PASSED BALL.

earned run average (ERA) – An important measure of a pitcher's effectiveness. The formula for computing earned run average is ER x IP / 9 (earned runs allowed times nine divided by innings pitched).

The lower the ERA the better. Normally, a pitcher is said to have a very good ERA if it is below 3.00, and an outstanding—*exceptionally* outstanding—ERA if it is below 2.00. The lowest ERA for a season in the modern era (1920–present) was 1.12 by Bob Gibson of the St. Louis Cardinals in 1968. To qualify for league leadership in ERA (and WHIP, too) a pitcher needs to have a minimum of 162 innings pitched (i.e., one for each game in his team's regular season schedule).

Elias Sports Bureau, Inc. – Founded in 1913, the Elias Sports Bureau, headquartered in New York City, is the official statistician for Major League Baseball. Each year they publish the 400-plus-page Elias Book of Baseball Records, used by baseball broadcasters throughout the country, sportswriters, and authors of baseball-themed books like the current one.

ERA – EARNED RUN AVERAGE. (ERA is technically an initialism, not an acronym, and is therefore pronounced *E-R-A,* not *era.*)

ERA+ – A measure of a pitcher's earned run average compared to the rest of the league, where 100 is average. The all-time ERA+ leader is New York Yankees relief pitcher Mariano Rivera, at 205, meaning, his career ERA was slightly over 100 percent better than the league career-average ERA. The starting pitcher with the all-time highest ERA+ as of this writing is Clayton Kershaw of the LA Dodgers, at 161, meaning his career ERA is 61 percent better than the league average. Here's the formula: 100*[lgERA/ERA] adjusted to the player's ballpark(s).

error – When in the judgment of the OFFICIAL SCORER a batted ball should have been fielded cleanly by a fielder—

but it was not and the batter reached base safely (or remained at bat in the case of a dropped foul ball)—the official scorer will charge the fielder (or fielders) involved in the play with an error. If a baserunner scores, the batter is *not* credited with an RBI.

extra-base hit – A hit that enables a batter to reach more than one base (i.e., a DOUBLE, TRIPLE, or HOME RUN).

extra innings – When a game is tied after the regulation nine innings, the teams play additional innings until one of them breaks the tie and wins the game. Eighty-two to eighty-five percent of tie games are resolved in three or fewer extra innings,[33] although some games can require many more. The most innings played in one game in MLB history was 26, a game between the Brooklyn Robins (aka Dodgers) and the Boston Braves, on May 1, 1920. The game was called due to darkness and ended in a 1-1 tie. The most innings played in an American League game was 25, between the White Sox and the Brewers, on May 8, 1984.

I was a pre-teen when I sat through a long extra-inning game in Oakland on September 6, 1969, when the Oakland A's battled the Minnesota Twins for 18 innings. The Twins finally prevailed, 8-6, and as a Twins fan, I was elated. Weary, but elated. I still have the scorecard from that five-hour, seventeen-minute game.

fair ball – A batted ball that lands on (or flies over) FAIR TERRITORY is a fair ball. However, a ball that lands in fair

---

[33] Based on research I conducted in the late 1990s using data from the *Sporting News Baseball Guides* for 1996, 1997, and 1998 and on stats I found online compiled by Devan Fink, who analyzed data from the 2012-2017 seasons (source: https://www.beyondtheboxscore.com/2017/8/5/16093390/extra-innings-time-how-long-how-many-average-rule-change)

territory between home and first base or third base and bounces or rolls into foul territory before it reaches the base is considered a foul ball.

fair territory – That part of the playing field bounded by the first base and third base lines

fan – In baseball, "fan" can be either a verb or a noun:

(1) fan (v.) – Used of a pitcher: to strike out a batter ("Clemens fanned 20 batters in a game during the 1986 season.")

   Used of a batter: to strike out. ("Cabrera fanned in his last at bat.")

(2) fan (n.) – A back formation or clipped form of *fanatic* (from the Latin *fanaticus*): An enthusiastic devotee, follower, or admirer of a sport or other activity. Another possibility is *fancier*, i.e., one who "fancies" a certain activity. First-known use for baseball devotees was in the mid-1880s. Cincinnati sports writer Ren Mulford Jr. is credited with popularizing the word.[34]

farm system – A network of minor league teams (also called "farm clubs") in which a big league club develops a talent pool from which to draw players for their 40-man ROSTER. Branch Rickey developed the first farm system while managing the St. Louis Cardinals in 1919. He later developed a farm system for the Brooklyn Dodgers. These were forerunners of today's farm systems, which all clubs have, that include minor league teams from the rookie

---

[34] Shulman 1996.

league level all the way to Triple-A, the highest minor league level before the majors.

fastball – See TYPES OF PITCHES.

fence (or outfield fence) – Sometimes called the "outfield wall." Ballparks did not always have a stationary outfield fence. In the mid- to late-nineteenth centuries, spectators often formed a human "wall" in the outfield. Outfield fences in stadiums today vary in height, but most are eight to ten feet high. A few fences are famous because of their uniqueness. For example, Boston's Fenway Park, home of the Red Sox, features the "Green Monster" in left field, which is 37 feet high and 231 feet long but only 310 feet from home plate. Chicago's Wrigley Field outfield fence is covered with Boston ivy; when a batted ball sticks in it, it is ruled a GROUND RULE DOUBLE.

fence buster – Hyperbolic slang for a SLUGGER who frequently hits baseballs deep to the outfield and over the fence. It's highly doubtful that any slugger in major league history has actually *busted* an outfield fence, but you never know.

fielder's choice – When a batter hits a ground ball to an infielder and there is at least one runner on base, the fielder theoretically has the choice of throwing to first to put out the base runner or throwing to the base ahead of the lead runner to try to put him out.

For example, with a runner on first, the batter hits a ground ball to the third baseman, who throws to second in time to put out (or force out—thus what's known as a FORCE PLAY) the runner coming from first. On the score card it is recorded that the batter reached first base on a 5–4 fielder's choice.[35]

fielding average (FA) (or fielding percentage) (a calculated statistic) – The formula for a fielder's fielding average is ERRORS/TOTAL CHANCES. The range for a fielding average is .000–1.000. In simplest terms, the fielding average is the percentage of total chances a fielder handles cleanly (without committing an error). For example, a shortstop whose fielding average is .958 has handled 95.8 percent of his total chances without an error, either in catching, scooping, throwing, or hanging onto the ball.

Baseball is the fabric of the American soul. The cliché goes: Baseball is as American as apple pie. I say more so. You can buy apple pie anywhere, but baseball is still a kid and his father shagging fly balls on a June afternoon at the park.

– Television host Larry King, from *What Baseball Means to Me,* edited by Curt Smith

---

Interesting fun fact: at the major league level, all team fielding averages are so high (generally between .940 and .960) that there is almost no statistical correlation between team fielding averages and WINNING PERCENTAGES. Of course, this doesn't mean that exceptional fielding ability isn't a consequential aspect of winning ballgames or that it isn't important. It is simply that the level of fielding from team to team in the majors over the course of a season is so consistently high that there is little statistical correlation to

---

[35] See SCOREKEEPING for further information.

winning. Certainly, other aspects of fielding also come into play, distinguishing the best teams from the rest, such as RANGE FACTOR.

fly ball/fly out (n.); **flies out** (v.) → **flied out**. We would say, "Johnson flied out to right field in the second inning and flied out to center in the fifth inning." It seems that it ought to be "flew out"—"Johnson flew out to right field"— but on further reflection we realize how grammatically absurd that would be. Johnson "flew out" to right field? Is Johnson a bird? Did Johnson magically sprout wings and fly out to right field? Or maybe he flew out on an airplane, helicopter, or hang-glider. Silly, of course. Johnson didn't do the flying—he hit a FLY BALL that was caught by an outfielder. He *flied out*, for pity's sake. Hey, just accept it—it's baseball!

force out/force play – A baserunner who is forced to leave his base by a batted ground ball may be put out at the base he is running toward. For example, Smith is on first and the batter, Jones, hits a fair ground ball (thus *forcing* Smith to run toward second base—he can't just decide to stay at first base, because there is a rule against two runners occupying the same base—and here comes the batter, charging up the base line). The ball is fielded by the shortstop, who throws to second before Smith arrives, thus *forcing* him out. The second baseman doesn't even need to tag Smith—only step on the base.

The force play is also called a **fielder's choice** because the fielder can make the split-second decision to attempt to force out the runner or, if he will throw to first, to put out the batter. In some situations, a runner who is not in a force situation will run for the next base on a ground ball when he doesn't have to. For example, runners are on first and third; the batter hits a ground ball to the second baseman who is playing in—meaning on or near the infield grass. The runner at third decides to try to score and he breaks for home. The second baseman may choose to throw to first to put out the batter, or he may throw to the catcher in an attempt to put out the runner coming from third. If he does so, the catcher will need to tag the runner with the ball. If successful, the announcer will say that the batter is safe at first on a fielder's choice, and in the scorebook it is scored something like "FC 4-2" (fielder's choice, base runner put out, second to catcher). In fact, even if the runner from third safely scored, the batter is still said to have reached base on a fielder's choice (not a base hit). In this case, it would be scored simply "FC."

foul/foul ball/foul tip – A batter who hits a ball that does not fall in fair territory is said to hit a foul (or foul ball). A foul ball is a strike, up to the second strike. After that, a batter can foul off pitches all day long and not strike out. The only time a batter makes an out by hitting a foul ball is when the ball is caught in the air, or when a batter with two strikes bunts a ball foul. The batter is out, and the pitcher is credited with a strikeout.

When a batter hits a foul ball sharply straight back into the catcher's mitt, it is called a **foul tip** and is a strike (not an out). However, if a batter with two strikes hits a foul tip, he is out (he has struck out).

foul line/pole – The white foul lines mark the boundaries for the playing field. One line extends from home plate to the left-field foul pole and one extends from home plate to the right-field foul pole. The lines intersect at home plate forming a right angle.

Batted balls that land outside the foul lines are foul balls. Balls that land in fair territory between home and first or between home and third and role or bounce into foul territory are also foul balls.

The foul poles are located where the foul lines intersect with the outfield fence. Their purpose is to aid umpires in determining whether fly balls over the fence are fair or foul. Poles must be at least 30 feet high, but 45 feet is recommended. A ball that strikes a foul pole on the fly is considered a home run.

foul territory – The part of the playing field outside the foul lines and behind home plate. In some ballparks, the foul territory is small and a relatively high percentage of foul balls fall out of play into the stands. Ballparks with small foul territories tend to favor the hitter because it's less likely a fielder will be able to catch foul balls. Ballparks with larger foul territories tend to favor the pitcher because more foul balls will be caught. Examples of ballparks with tiny foul territories are Wrigley Field in Chicago and Fenway Park in Boston. Parks with large foul territories include the Oakland Alameda Stadium and Comerica Park in Detroit.

four-bagger – A HOME RUN.

frame – Another word for inning. ("Through the end of the third frame, the Padres lead the Cubs, 3–2.")

free pass – A base on balls (walk).

friendly confines – The home ballpark.

fungo – A fly ball hit for fielding practice. A coach tosses up the ball and hits it into the air with a long, narrow bat.

games behind/games back (GB) – In the standings, GB refers to how far back a team is from the division or league leader. To derive GB, follow these four simple steps: (1) subtract a trailing team's wins from the leading team's wins; (2) subtract the leading team's losses from the trailing team's losses; (3) add those two numbers; (4) divide the sum by two. For example, as I write this, in the AL Central division, Cleveland is in first place with a record of 67-51. Minnesota is in second, at 54-63, 12.5 games behind. Subtract Cleveland's 54 wins from Minnesota's 67 wins (= 13); subtract Minnesota's 51 losses from Cleveland's 63 losses (= 12); add those together (13+12 = 25); divide by two (= 12.5). Easy—even for a non-mathematical guy like me.

gap, the – The relatively spacious area of the outfield between center and left field or center and right field. A ball hit "into the gap" will often fall in for a double or, if the batter is fleet of foot, a triple.

"Gee! It's a Wonderful Game" – The title of one of the many popular Tin Pan Alley hit baseball songs of the early 20th century with a seriously catchy tune. Featured in Ken Burns's *Baseball* documentary series.[36]

general manager – The team executive in the front office who is in charge of the overall operation of the ball club.

glass arm – A pitcher's sore or fragile arm, susceptible to fatigue or injury.

---

[36] Included here because it was originally to be the title of this book. Baseball is indeed a "wonderful game"—but my son convinced me that readers today might not appreciate such an old-timey reference. I think it was "Gee!" that killed it for him, and I agreed. Thus, the present title.

glove, baseball – Fielders' gloves were first widely used in 1875, one year prior to the founding of the National League. Special mitts for catchers were introduced in the 1880s. Initially, fielders' gloves were not much more than regular leather gloves, padded to protect a player's hand. As the game and its equipment evolved, gloves grew in size, webbing was added, and they became tools to help players catch the ball better.

GO/AO – The ratio of a batter's GROUND OUTS to AIR OUTS.

Golden Age (or Era) of baseball – Depending on who you talk to, the "Golden Age" of baseball occurred in the 1930s—or maybe the '40s, or possibly the '50s, or the '60s—when players were heroic figures who played for love and for the thrill of it; when baseball was still king of all sports and the undisputed National Pastime.

Was there really a Golden Age—one epoch in history when the sport was somehow better, somehow more quintessentially *baseball* than all others? Older fans (like the author), overcome with nostalgia, often think of a time "away back when"—in the "good ol' days"—when the only way to follow a ball game in real time was to tune in to it on AM radio (if you were fortunate enough to live in the broadcast region) or watch it on NBC's "Game of the Week" on Saturday afternoon. In my small town in the Midwest, updated batting and pitching stats for most players were published in the local newspaper once a week, on Sunday. I loved poring over those columns of black-and-white names and numbers, soaking up Killebrew's home run totals, Clemente's batting average, Brock's stolen bases, Yastrzemski's RBIs, and Koufax's wins, earned run average, strikeouts (and just about everything else). For me, that could have been *the* Golden Age of baseball.

And yet, maybe *your* "golden age" is nestled in your own early memories—when you first watched a ballgame sitting on your dad's or big brother's lap; when you first thrilled to the sights, sounds, smells, and tastes of a big league stadium; when you opened a pack of baseball cards and discovered your very favorite player; when you played ball with the neighborhood boys in a vacant lot on warm summer evenings until it was too dark to see the ball; when you played catch with your dad in your backyard.

Maybe *your* "golden age of baseball" is the one that really matters.

If asked where baseball stood amid such notions as country, family, love, honor, art, and religion, we might say derisively, "Just a game." But, under oath, I'd abandon some of those Big Six before I'd give up baseball.

– Thomas Boswell

Gold Glove Award – The managers and coaches of major league teams vote for the best fielder at each position in their respective leagues near the end of the season.[37] Various fielding factors are considered, such as a player's FIELDING AVERAGE, RANGE FACTOR, and throwing ability. The top vote-getters are presented the Gold Glove Award, sponsored by the Rawlings

---

[37] Accordingly, there are nine award recipients in the NL and nine in the AL. Managers and coaches may not vote for players on their own teams.

Sporting Goods Company since 1957. The award trophy is a glove or mitt made of gold-finished leather and mounted on a wooden stand with an engraved plate. Award recipients are called "Gold Glovers." An American League player whose primary role is DESIGNATED HITTER is not eligible to receive a Gold Glove.[38]

gopher ball – A HOME RUN. The term presumably originated in the early days of baseball when a long-hit ball bounded or rolled beyond the playing field (which often had no fence) and a fielder had to run and retrieve it—or "go fer it." Or perhaps it referred to the way such a long-hit ball would vanish out of sight, like a gopher disappearing into its hole.

go the distance –An expression that refers to a starting pitcher pitching a COMPLETE GAME. "Go the distance" is one of the iconic lines in the book and movie *Field of Dreams*, in which Ray Kinsella hears a mysterious voice tell him to build a ball diamond in his Iowa cornfield. The other line from the movie that is now so well known that it has entered into the American vernacular is, "If you build it, he will come."

go yard/went yard – A popular but grammatically incorrect expression catching on among sports writers and broadcasters in recent years, meaning "to hit the ball out of the yard," or "hit a HOME RUN."

goose egg – Slang term for the number zero. Often used when a pitcher gives up no runs in an inning—he is said to have put up a goose egg.

---

38 That's a "duh," right? But I don't want to assume it's obvious to everyone.

After all, a goose egg does have a faint resemblance to the number zero.

grand slam – As a kid I thought a grand slam was a powerfully smacked home run that sailed way, way over the outfield fence. A monster wallop hit by a musclebound slugger. It is not. A grand slam is a home run (or, a "slam") hit with the BASES LOADED, thus scoring four runs, the maximum possible produced by a BASE HIT (which makes it "simply grand").

Alex Rodriguez, who played for the Mariners, Rangers, and Yankees, holds the major league record for career grand slams with 25, hit between 1994 and 2016. The most grand slams ever slugged in a single season is 6, a record achieved by Don Mattingly of the New York Yankees in 1987, and equaled by Travis Hafner of the Cleveland Indians in 2006.

grass-cutter – A hard-hit ground ball that stays low and does not hop or bounce. Sometimes called a DAISY CUTTER or LAWN MOWER.

Green Monster – The gigantic left field wall in baseball's oldest stadium, Fenway Park, Boston. It is 37 feet tall and 231 feet long.

ground ball/grounder – A batted ball that is hit on the ground.

ground out – a GROUND BALL that is fielded cleanly by  (usually—well, almost always) an infielder who puts out the batter by stepping on first base or tagging the batter, or by throwing to another infielder who steps on first base or tags the runner. The term also applies to FORCE OUTS.

ground-rule double – A two-base hit credited when a batter hits a fair ball that hits the ground and bounces over the outfield fence, or, as in the case of Chicago's Wrigley Field, that becomes lodged in the ivy that covers the outfield fence (or, as in the case of Boston's Fenway Park, goes through the scoreboard on the GREEN MONSTER, either on the fly or the bound). The batter must stop at second base and any baserunners may advance exactly two bases.

Hall of Fame, National Baseball – By the mid-1930s, major league baseball had existed for more than sixty years, and a growing number of ballplayers had become household names through their achievements on the playing field. The National Baseball Hall of Fame was established in Cooperstown, New York, in 1936 to honor the greatest figures associated with the game.

The first five inductees were Ty Cobb, Babe Ruth, Christy Mathewson, Honus Wagner, and Walter Johnson. To be eligible for induction, a player must have played in a minimum of ten seasons and have been retired a minimum of five years. Players are nominated and elected by the Baseball Writers Association of America (BBWAA), although a special Veterans Committee occasionally selects players from years past who they deem deserving of the honor.

As of this writing, 317 individuals have been inducted into the HOF, a list that includes players, managers, umpires, and executives (in the latter group is the one-and-only woman in the HOF, Effa Manley, a Negro League executive, who was elected in 2006).

hand out – In baseball's earliest days, an OUT or PUTOUT was originally a "hand out." I can imagine that to avoid confusion with a "handout" (i.e., a freebie), it was just simpler to call it an "out."

hit – same as BASE HIT.

hit-and-run play – With a speedy runner on first, or on first and third—usually with less than two outs and a good CONTACT HITTER up to bat—a manager may call for the hit-and-run play. As the pitcher delivers his pitch, the baserunner breaks for the next base. The batter attempts to make contact with the ball and preferably hit it to the right side of the diamond. If successful, and he grounds out to the second baseman, the runner on first will likely make it safely to second; if the ball fortuitously scoots past the infielder for a base hit, the baserunner will invariably make it at least to third base and possibly even score a run—on a single.

My favorite play is the hit and run. See who's covering [the bag] and hit a ground ball where he was.

– Tony Gwynn (8-time NL batting champ)

---

hit by pitch (HBP) – When a player at bat is hit by a pitcher's errant pitch, he is awarded first base immediately. If the bases were loaded, a run will score and the batter is credited with a RUN BATTED IN (RBI). A batter hit by a pitch is not credited with an at-bat.

hitters' park – A ballpark that consistently features higher team SLASH LINES and more runs produced than the league average may be known as a "hitters' park." The possible causes include shorter distances to the outfield fence, smaller foul territories (where more foul balls end up in the stands, thus helping hitters to "stay alive" with additional opportunities to get on base hit), wind that tends to blow out toward the outfield, and thinner air (such as at Coors Field in the mile-high city of Denver, Colorado). Any one or a combination of such factors often lead to higher scoring games than average for the league.

hit for the cycle – A rare feat in major league baseball, a batter who hits a single, double, triple, and home run (in any order) in the same game has hit for the cycle. As of this writing, the feat has been accomplished 302 times in major league history. Several players have done it two times, but only two have done so three times: Bob Meusel of the Yankees (1921, 1922 & 1928) and Adrian Beltre of the Mariners (2008) and the Rangers (2012 & 2015). When a batter hits the cycle in order: a single, then a double, then a triple, and finally a home run—it is called a "natural cycle," which has occurred only 13 times in major league history.

hit the showers – When a pitcher is pulled from the game because he's having trouble hitting the strike zone, or he has given up too many hits or walks, and therefore too many runs, the announcer might say, "The manager is calling for a new pitcher from the bullpen and Pete will hit the showers. His day is done." Once a player is removed from a game for a substitute, he may not return to the field or the batting lineup until the next game.

hitting streak – The number of consecutive games in which a player has at least one BASE HIT. Announcers may begin to mention it when a batter racks up a hitting streak of 10 or more games. A streak is especially worth mentioning when it reaches 20 games. Most players—even very good hitters—will play their entire career without notching a hitting streak of 20 games. The longest hitting streak in National League history was Wee Willie Keeler's 45-game streak in 1896-97. Pete Rose produced a 44-game streak while playing for the Cincinnati Reds in 1978. But the distinction of the longest hitting streak in American League and major league history belongs to Joe DiMaggio of the New York Yankees, who in 1941 hit safely in 56 consecutive games, a record that has stood, unapproached, for over 75 years.

It's a game for the whole family, so let's all forget our worries and have fun at the ball game whenever we can get to one.
What do you say?
Let's go!

– Actor William Frawley in an early 1950s commercial made for movie theaters

---

hold – An unofficial pitching statistic that first appeared in 1987. A relief pitcher who enters a game in a SAVE OPPORTUNITY and leaves the game before its conclusion with his team still ahead is said to "hold" the lead.

holding the runner – When a runner is on base and an infielder stations himself close to the base to potentially field a pickoff attempt by the pitcher or the catcher, the defense is said to be holding the runner close to the base. Generally the baserunner will not take a lengthy lead if the infielder is holding him, which reduces the likelihood of his stealing a base or advancing to the next base successfully on a ground ball or fly ball.

home or **home plate** (officially, **home base**) – Since 1900, home base (or home plate) has been a five-sided figure seventeen inches wide.

home run – A batter is credited with a home run and a free pass around the bases when he hits a fair ball over the outfield fence. The batter and any base runners are allowed to freely circle the bases, being careful to step on each base, and score a run by stepping on home plate. A home run is also credited when the batter is able to circle the bases and score a run on a fair ball that does not clear the outfield fence. This is called an "inside-the-park" home run. Inside-the-park home runs are exciting to watch but extremely uncommon in the major leagues.

Babe Ruth

The home run is perhaps the most exciting play in baseball, typically bringing the home town fans to their feet in wild celebration while the batting hero takes his 15-second jog around the bases. Home run sluggers are the titans of baseball, heroes to their devoted fans and the team executives who live to fill their stadiums with devoted fans. The first, and possibly greatest, home run titan was George Herman "Babe" Ruth, who began his career as a pitcher for the Boston Red Sox during World War I and then spent the bulk of his career as an outfielder with the New York Yankees, rewriting the home-run record book and single-handedly revitalizing major league baseball.

The all-time single-season home run record is 73, set by Barry Bonds of the San Francisco Giants in 2001. Bonds's feat surpassed Mark McGwire's 70 home runs in 1998, which at the time established the new record that demolished Roger Maris's single-season record of 61, set in 1961. Bonds also holds the all-time home run record, with 762. Bonds and McGwire (and others of that late-'90s–early 2000s era) were accused of using performance enhancing drugs (PEDs) to artificially pump up their muscles and their home run totals. Some observers argue that any records potentially related to steroid use (such as home runs, total bases, and slugging percentage) should be disavowed by MLB, or at least marked with asterisks and footnoted. Although I tend to agree with those observers (in my mind the all-time home run king is still Hank Aaron, who "went yard" 755 times in the non-steroid era), for the purposes of this book I am merely reporting the official MLB records.

In major league history, 18 players have hit four home runs in a game. The last to do so was J.D. Martinez of the Arizona Diamondbacks on September 4, 2017. No player has hit more than four in one game.

Home run hitting is, overall, on the upswing in MLB (no pun intended). Collectively, players hit more homers in 2017 than in any other year in history. (There were also astoundingly high totals of strikeouts and walks in 2017. See THREE TRUE OUTCOMES.)

There are many slang terms and colorful expressions for the home run. Here's a non-exhaustive list of twenty of them for your entertainment:

1. *big fly*
2. *blast*
3. *bomb*
4. *circuit clout*
5. *canon shot*
6. *dinger*
7. *four-bagger*
8. *goner*
9. *gopher ball*
10. *go yard* (past tense: *went yard*) – Although grammatically peculiar, it is gaining in popularity.
11. *grand salami* – for a GRAND SLAM, obviously.
12. *homer* – Understandably, the most common nickname for a home run. Can be either a noun ("Harper hit a homer to deep left") or a verb, typically in past tense ("Trout has homered in three consecutive games.")
13. *jack*
14. *long ball*
15. *moon shot*
16. *round tripper*
17. *shot*
18. *slam*
19. *souvenir* (see SOUVENIR FOR A LUCKY FAN)
20. *tater*

hot dog – The traditional baseball sandwich sold at ballparks since the very early twentieth century. Actor Humphrey Bogart once famously said, "A hot dog at the ballpark is better than a steak at the Ritz."

immaculate inning – An inning in which a pitcher retires the side on three straight strikeouts, with nine consecutive strikes. The unusual feat has occurred only 93 times in major league history.

infield – The area of the playing field within the confines of the diamond itself, demarcated by the first- and third-baselines and the area (usually consisting of dirt) between first and second base and between second and third base.

infield fly rule – With less than two outs and runners on first and second base, or on first, second, and third bases, a batter who hits a pop fly to the infield is immediately called out. This is to prevent an infielder from deceiving the baserunners by allowing the ball to drop to the ground and thereby turn an easy double play, which happened quite frequently before the rule was adopted in 1894.

inning – Baseball is the only major team sport not played according to timed periods. It is played according to innings, of which there are nine, unless the game is shortened due to inclement weather or extended due to a tie. An inning consists of six outs—three by the visiting team, which always bats first, and three by the home team, which always bats second.

intentional walk/base on balls – (Sometimes called a "free pass.") Occasionally, the defensive team's manager makes the strategic decision that a batter should be put on first base—usually when first base is open—and will signal for the pitcher to intentionally walk the batter. Until the 2017 season, a pitcher would need to throw four pitches to the catcher, who would step three or four feet to one side of home plate as the pitcher delivered the ball to ensure that the pitches were well outside the strike zone—and outside the reach of the batter. After four such pitches, the batter was awarded first base.

In an effort to keep the game moving along, starting with the 2017 season a manager simply announces his intention to walk a batter, and the umpire awards first base to the batter without a pitch being thrown.

Why would a manager choose to intentionally walk a batter? If the game is close, first base is open, and a dangerous hitter is up to bat, the manager may want to take the bat out of the hitter's hands by walking him. A second purpose is to set up a potential double play when there are fewer than two outs and, again, first base is open. With two outs and a runner on second, or runners on second and third, another reason to issue an intentional walk is to set up a potential force out at second and third (or second, third, and home).

Typically, it is heavy hitters who are most inclined to be intentionally walked. The record for most free passes received in a season belongs to all-time home run king Barry Bonds of the San Francisco Giants, who was intentionally walked 120 times in 2004.[39] Bonds also holds the career record with 688 intentional walks.

interleague play – Until June 12, 1997, the only occasions when a team from the National League played a team from the American League were the All-Star Game, the World Series, and the occasional exhibition game, such as those

---

[39] To put this figure in perspective, Bonds's 120 intentional walks in 2004 were 23 more than Alex Rodriguez, who is fifth on the all-time home run list, received *in his entire 22-year career.*

played during spring training. But on that date in 1997, the San Francisco Giants of the NL traveled to Arlington, Texas, to play the Texas Rangers of the AL in the first-ever regular-season interleague game. While baseball purists (like yours truly) object to interleague play during the regular season, the rationale does make some sense: it provides opportunities for fans in National League cities to see American League stars play, and vice versa. And that should bring more fans to the ballpark. More fans in the ballpark means more revenue generated. Get it? It's pretty simple.

iron glove – Like WOODEN GLOVE, an unflattering term for the fielding ability of a player who fields, well, unflatteringly. He has a reputation for dropping, bobbling, booting, or otherwise misplaying batted balls.

Jackie Robinson Award – Since 1987 the official name for the ROOKIE OF THE YEAR AWARD. Playing second base for the Brooklyn Dodgers, Robinson, the first recipient in 1947, not only braved the prejudice and hatred of major leaguers, sportswriters, and members of the general public as the first African American ballplayer to break the color barrier—a feat which alone qualified him to win major recognition—but he performed astonishingly well. He batted .297 with 12 home runs, 48 RBIs, 125 runs scored, and a league-leading 29 stolen bases in 151 games.

In recognition of Robinson's dual achievement, the Baseball Writers Association of America (BWAA) created the award at the conclusion of the 1947 season to recognize superior performance by that rookie. Since 1949, MLB has awarded the ROY to the top rookie in each league.

jump – A baserunner is said to get a jump on the pitcher when he breaks for the next open base in a steal attempt while the pitcher is delivering his pitch.

junior circuit – The AMERICAN LEAGUE, the younger of the two major leagues.

There are two theories on hitting the knuckleball. Unfortunately, neither of them works.

– Hitting instructor Charlie Lau

---

knuckleball – A pitch in which the pitcher grips the ball typically with fingertips or knuckles. It is a slower pitch, thrown with virtually no spin, which causes the ball to flutter unpredictably, making it difficult to hit . . . and catch. A handful of major league pitchers throw it exclusively and are known as "knuckleball pitchers." Because the pitch puts a relatively small amount of stress on a pitcher's arm, good knuckleball pitchers often play much longer than other pitchers—often well into their forties. Notable knuckleball pitchers in history have been Hall-of-Famers Phil Niekro (who pitched until he was 48 and won 318 games) and Hall of Fame reliever Hoyt Wilhelm (who pitched until age 49, appearing in 1070 games).

lawn mower – A hard-hit ground ball. (Same as GRASS CUTTER.)

lead – This isn't about one team having more runs than the other. It's a base-running term that refers to the baserunner stepping off his base and taking one or more steps toward the next base while the pitcher is preparing to hurl his next pitch. Taking a lead is completely legal in major league baseball. Many youth leagues prohibit taking a lead—baserunners must remain in contact with their

---

The best way to catch a knuckleball is to wait until the ball stops rolling and then pick it up.

–Bob Uecker, former big league
catcher and broadcaster

---

bases until the pitcher is actually throwing the ball toward the batter. Then the runner can leave his base. But in the majors, aggressive baserunners will sometimes take sizable leads to distract the pitcher or dare him to attempt a PICKOFF. Often, the baserunners who take the biggest leads are known for their propensity to STEAL bases.

leadoff hitter – The first batter in a team's LINEUP. Historically, managers have generally made batters with healthy on-base averages (OBAs) the leadoff hitter.

line drive/liner – A solidly hit ball that stays off the ground, with little to no arc, and often falls in for a base hit, but sometimes is caught by an alert infielder or outfielder. Line drives hit into the outfield GAP or down the baselines frequently result in EXTRA-BASE HITs.

line score – The summary of a team's runs, hits, and errors made in a game. Often, the linescore will also include the inning-by-inning runs scored by each team. The visiting team, which bats first, is always on top in a line score, and the home team, which always bats second, is on the bottom. Here's an example of a linescore (with apologies to my Giants-fan readers). You will note in this example an x appears in the bottom of the ninth inning for Los Angeles, the home team. Here's why. If the home team is ahead after the visiting team has batted in the top of the ninth inning, the game is over; the home team has won, so there's no need to bat in the bottom of the FRAME. The last three columns are RUNS, HITS, and ERRORS.

San Francisco Giants	*000*	*001*	*000*	*1*	*5*	*2*
Los Angeles Dodgers	*100*	*203*	*00x*	*6*	*11*	*0*

If you're watching the game on television or online, the linescore typically appears in a corner of the screen and is usually abbreviated, something like this:

SF	*1*	*5*	*2*
LA	*6*	*11*	*0*

Or it may depict only the score, with other information

such as who's pitching and who's batting, the inning (and whether it's the top of the inning or the bottom of the inning), the count (i.e., balls and strikes), runners on base (if any) and how many outs.

lineup – The order in which a team's players bat. The lineup must remain the same throughout the game, meaning that Joe Smith can't play a couple of innings batting third and then move up to second or down to fifth; however, the manager may make substitutions in the lineup with pinch hitters, pinch runners, pitching changes, or defensive (fielding position) changes. Once a player is removed from the lineup for a substitute, he may no longer play in that game.

little ball (or small ball) – A term to describe a team strategy of aggressive play where teams rely on "little" plays to move baserunners around the base paths, such as HIT-AND-RUNS, STOLEN BASES, SACRIFICE HITS, even ground-ball outs hit to the right (second base) side of the infield. Most teams in the infamous Deadball Era depended on little-ball strategy because pitching was dominant, home runs were infrequent, and runs were generally hard to come by. In the modern era, individual managers have built successful teams with little ball (combined with solid pitching). For example, in 1985 manager Whitey Herzog's St. Louis Cardinals hit just 87 home runs but stole 314 bases in winning the NL pennant.

Little League® Baseball – Although kids have played baseball since its origins, the highly structured national organization known as Little League was started in 1939 in Williamsport, PA, by Carl E. Stotz, a tax collector. For the first 35 years of its existence, only boys were allowed to play, but a court order in 1974 allowed girls to

---

Little League baseball is a very good thing because it keeps the parents off the streets.

– Yogi Berra, quoted in *Catcher in the Wry* by Bob Uecker

---

participate.[40] My own son played Little League ball from tee ball (age six) through "majors" (age eleven). I helped as a coach a couple of years and served as the team scorekeeper and statistician for another couple of years. My daughter played Bobby Sox softball (not affiliated with Little League) for a couple of years as well.

In my own experience, as a ten-year-old kid, I played in a city youth league that wasn't technically "Little League," but it was the closest thing to it in my small town in Colorado. I wasn't much of a player. More specifically, I was a *terrible* hitter, but I had a decent glove and could catch fly balls, so I played in the outfield. I'm sure the coach cringed whenever I stepped into the batter's box. Although I couldn't hit, I could take pitches, and the few times I got on base that summer was because I walked. In my one moment of near glory, there were two outs in the bottom of the last inning, with the potential tying run on third base. With the count full at three balls and two strikes, the PAYOFF PITCH was a fat, juicy, grapefruit.[41] I knew I was going to blast it to kingdom come. In my mind I could hear the crack of the bat as its sweet spot met the ball with terrific force; I could feel the impact in my hands as the wood made contact with cowhide; I could see the ball streaking over the shortstop's head into left field—no, over the left field fence (I was freaking Harmon Killebrew!). In that brief instant I knew I would be that day's hero. But, as in every other time I swung at a pitch that summer, I missed the ball. Strike three. Game over. (Cue the violin.)

---

[40] Dickson 2009, 509.
[41] A "grapefruit" is a slow-moving pitch that the batter thinks is ripe for belting into the stratosphere.

Today Little League baseball is as popular as ever, parents investing money, time, sweat, and tears in their son or daughter's chance at stardom. The season culminates every August in the Little League World Series played at Bowman Field in Williamsport, PA.

LOB – The box score abbreviation for [runners] left on base. A player who safely reaches base during an inning and is unable to score before the third out is said to be "left on base." Since the object of a team's "ups" each inning is to get on base and score runs, leaving runners on base is the antithesis of that object. Theoretically, during a nine-inning game a team may leave anywhere from zero to 27 baserunners on base—the latter (leaving the bases loaded at the end of every inning) has never happened in a major league game. The record for most runners left on base during a 9-inning game is 20, by the New York Yankees vs. the Boston Red Sox, on 9/21/1956. Over a recent ten-season stretch (2007-2016) the average number of runners left on base per game per team was 7. (Exactly 6.97, for those who must have more precision in order to sleep at night.)

lollipop –An easy-to-hit soft pitch or a weak throw.

long ball – A HOME RUN.

looking – A batter can strike out either by swinging or "looking"—the latter when he fails to swing at strike three, looking at it as it flies past him. Scorekeepers often distinguish between the two in the scorebook by writing K for a swinging strikeout and a backwards K for a "looking" strikeout.

"Maddux" – A relatively recent term, coined by blogger Jason Lukehart, to describe a pitcher's complete-game shutout in which he throws fewer than 100 pitches—after Hall of Fame pitcher Greg Maddux, who accomplished the feat 13 times in his career. Lukehart adds this information: "Madduxes are fairly rare. There have been an average of roughly eleven per season going back to 1988, when MLB pitch counts began to be kept consistently. There are 306 Madduxes on record since then, thrown by 194 different pitchers."[42] Greg Maddux's 13 "Madduxes" are by far the most by any pitcher since 1988.

magic number – The combined number of a first-place team's wins and the second-place team's losses needed for the first-place team to clinch the division title. The formula for calculating the magic number is the number of first-place team's games remaining minus the second-place team's games behind. For example, say team Y is in first place with a record of 90-61 and team X is in second place, 6 games behind with a record of 85-68. Team Y has 11 games remaining, minus Team X's 6 games behind, equals a magic number of 5. What this means is that if Team Y wins just five of its remaining 11 games it would claim the division title, even if Team X won all 9 of its remaining games. (Team Y finishes at 95-67 and Team X finishes at 94-68.) Another scenario would be Team Y losing all 11 of its final games, but with Team X losing just 5 games, Team Y still takes home the trophy. (Team Y finishes at 90-72 and Team X finishes at 89-73). If Team Y is your favorite team, with a magic number of 5, it's fun to watch the final games unfold. If Team Y wins today's game and Team X

---

[42] Lukehart introduced the term in his blog on April 18, 2012 (groundballwitheyes.blogspot.com/2012/04/maddux.html). He has attempted to keep the list of Madduxes current since then.

loses today's game, the magic number is reduced by 2 (it's now 3).

manager –The term usually refers to the field manager, the man in charge of the players and coaches. He is responsible for developing, training, motivating, and directing the players; he determines the lineups for each game; he directs the game strategy; he decides if and when to pull pitchers and who to bring in from the bull pen; he calls for pinch hitters and pinch runners. He wears a uniform and remains in the dugout during the game—unless he goes onto the field to confer with his pitcher or question a call by an umpire. His continued employment with the team often depends on how well his team does in the standings, and some owners change managers as often as they change their socks.

The secret of managing a club is to keep the five guys who hate you away from the five who are undecided.

– Legendary manager Casey Stengel

Mendoza Line – A batting average of .200 or lower— considered exceptionally low for a position player in the major leagues. The term was coined as a joke in 1979 by a teammate of light-hitting Seattle Mariners shortstop Mario Mendoza, who typically batted around .200. Although Mendoza actually had a career average of .215, he did bat less than .200 in five of his nine big league seasons.

modern era – Baseball history can be divided into roughly three eras: (1) the early era (1870s to 1899) when rules and playing field dimensions were constantly in flux; (2) the DEADBALL ERA (1900 to 1919) when balls were frequently dirty (from spitballs and overuse), when ballpark dimensions were more expansive (making it difficult to hit home runs, but easier to hit triples), and when playing LITTLE BALL was definitely in vogue. All of this tended to keep batting averages and earned run averages low; and (3) the modern era (1920 to the present).[43] The big change between 1919 and 1920 was the introduction of a livelier baseball and, by the end of 1920—after Ray Chapman's death by BEANING—the practice of umpires keeping fresher, cleaner, whiter balls in play that batters could see more clearly. Hitters' batting and slugging averages and pitchers' earned run averages saw a dramatic increase in the years after 1920. Players hit more home runs. Babe Ruth kicked off the age of the long ball in dramatic fashion in 1920, when his 54 taters were more than were hit by any other *team* in the American League, and more than seven of the eight National League teams. It could be argued that, since around 2010, we are seeing a fourth era in baseball: the era of the "THREE TRUE OUTCOMES" (walks, strikeouts, and home runs).

Most Valuable Player Award – The earliest formal recognition of a single player as the league's "most valuable" in a given season occurred in 1911, when the Chalmers Motor Company of Detroit awarded an automobile to the player determined by a committee of baseball writers to have been "the most important and useful player to the club and to the league" that season.[44]

---

[43] There is no uniform agreement on these three categories and the time frames. All are endlessly disputed by baseball experts and fans.

[44] https://en.wikipedia.org/wiki/Major_League_Baseball_

Ty Cobb of the Detroit Tigers and Frank Schulte of the Chicago Cubs were the AL and NL winners respectively. Chalmers discontinued the award after the 1914 season.

In 1922, a second attempt at honoring each league's top player resulted in the League Award, which died in 1930. Finally, the Baseball Writers' Association of America assumed the role of selecting each league's most valuable player, which has continued without interruption each year from 1931 to the present with the award known simply as the Most Valuable Player Award (or MVP). The first AL MVP award, in 1931, was given to pitcher Lefty Grove of the Philadelphia Athletics—some 25 years before the first CY YOUNG AWARD was given to each year's top pitcher(s). Although a pitcher can win *both* the MVP and Cy Young Awards—and several have—this writer is of the opinion that the MVP should go to POSITION PLAYERS only.

mound, the – See PITCHER'S MOUND.

If you build it, he will come.

The "Voice" in *Field of Dreams* (1989)

---

movies, baseball-related – Baseball has served as the subject of, or backdrop to, dozens of feature films and thousands of books. According to Forbes.com, the top five

Most_Valuable_Player_Award#Chalmers_Award_(1911%E2%80%93191 4) (Retrieved 8/31/18)

grossing baseball-themed movies since 1982 are as follows (with year released in parentheses)[45]:

1. *A League of Their Own* (1992) – A fictional, humorous, and poignant account of the real-life All-American Girls' Professional Baseball League that was founded in 1943. (See WOMEN'S PROFESSIONAL BASEBALL.) Directed by Penny Marshall.

2. *42* (2013) – The true story of Jackie Robinson, one of the most inspirational figures in baseball history, who broke the color barrier in 1947.

3. *Moneyball* (2011) – Based on the true story of how Oakland A's general manager Billy Beane utilized a revolutionary new concept in 1999 to turn a weak, sub-.500 ball club and turn it into a pennant contender that made the playoffs four consecutive years (2000-2003). Starring Brad Pitt as Billy Beane.

4. *The Rookie* (2002) – Based on the true story of high school baseball coach Jim Morris, who made it to the big leagues as a pitcher, against all odds, as a 35-year-old rookie in 1999.

5. *Field of Dreams* (1989) – The fictional account of how dreams come true in an Iowa cornfield for a disgraced ballplayer (Shoeless Joe Jackson), a doctor ("Moonlight" Graham), a city-slicker-turned-farmer (Ray Kinsella), and a bitter, once-famous author (Terence Mann). Starring Kevin Costner, James Earl Jones, Ray Liotta,

---

45 www.forbes.com/sites/gabezaldivar/2016/03/31/power-ranking-the-11-highest-grossing-baseball-movies-of-all-time/#457b94387138 (Retrieved 8/12/18)

and Burt Lancaster. It's my all-time personal favorite, and a real tearjerker for many men (the author included).

Here is the Rotten Tomatoes® ranking of the all-time top ten baseball movies and year of release[46]:

1. *Bull Durham* (1988) – Starring Kevin Costner and Susan Sarandon.

2. *Moneyball* (2011) – See synopsis above.

3. *The Life and Times of Hank Greenberg* (2000) – Documentary on Jewish baseball great Hank Greenberg, who pioneered Jewish integration into major league baseball during the Depression and World War II.

4. *The Bad News Bears* (1976) – One of the first kids' sports comedies, starring Walter Matthau and Tatum O'Neal.

5. *The Pride of the Yankees* (1942) – The story of the great New York Yankees "Iron Horse," Lou Gehrig, who contracted Amyotrophic Lateral Sclerosis (ALS—which became "Lou Gehrig's Disease") and died a young man after a phenomenal career in which he set the record for consecutive games played, at 2,130, which stood for over 56 years. Starring Gary Cooper.

6. *Sugar* (2008) – A fictional tale about a talented young ballplayer from the Dominican Republic who yearns to break into the major leagues. Starring Algenis Perez Soto.

7. *Up for Grabs* (2005) – A documentary about two men who laid claim to Barry Bonds's record-setting 73rd home

---

[46] Retrieved 8/12/18 from
www.rottentomatoes.com/guides/best_baseball_movies/

run, hit in San Francisco in 2001, and their ensuing legal battles.

8. *Field of Dreams* (1989). – See synopsis above.

9. *Bang the Drum Slowly* (1973) – Fictional story based on the classic novel of the same name by Mark Harris, about a quirky, naïve misfit catcher who struggles for acceptance by his teammates. Starring Robert DeNiro and Michael Moriarty.

10. *Eight Men Out* (1988) – Based on the true story of the infamous 1919 "Black Sox" scandal that nearly ruined major league baseball. Starring John Cusack, Charlie Sheen, and D.B. Sweeney.

In addition to these popular films, I would be remiss if I failed to mention the Ken Burns ten-part documentary masterpiece, *Baseball: A Film by Ken Burns*. Highly recommended. Other personal favorites are *The Natural* (1984), starring Robert Redford, and *For Love of the Game* (1999), starring Kevin Costner.

music of baseball – No sport in America has inspired more music than baseball, which was true almost from the start. In 1858, J. R. Blodgett composed and published "The Baseball Polka." Since then, the sheet music for more than 420 baseball-themed songs have made their way into the Library of Congress. In 1908, Albert Von Tilzer composed the tune and Jack Norworth the lyrics of a Tin Pan Alley hit that would soon become the unofficial song of the national game, "Take Me Out to the Ballgame." Today, according to the Library of Congress, it is the third most popular song in America, behind "Happy Birthday" and "The Star-Spangled Banner." It is traditionally sung during the SEVENTH INNING STRETCH at major- and minor-league

84

ballparks in America, although since 9/11, "God Bless America" is frequently sung instead.

Other popular baseball songs through the decades include "Hurrah for the National Game" (1868), "Gee! It's a Wonderful Game" (1911), "If You Can't Make a Hit in the Ball Game (You can't make a hit with me)" (1912), "Joltin' Joe DiMaggio (1941), "Did You See Jackie Robinson Hit That Ball?" (1949), and "Baseball Boogie" (1977).

National Anthem – As baseball has been the National Game since its earliest days, it isn't surprising that the hyper-patriotic "Star-Spangled Banner," composed in 1814, came to be associated with it. Sporadic newspaper reports of the song being played or sung at big league ball games date as far back as the 1860s, long before it became America's National Anthem in 1931. However, it wasn't until just before World War II that all major league teams were playing it before every game.

National Association – The first professional baseball league in America. Established in 1871, the National Association (NA) consisted of nine teams, playing schedules ranging from 25 to 33 games. Never highly organized, teams came and went, and schedules were inconsistent. It disbanded after five seasons, which cleared the way for a new league to form in 1876—the NATIONAL LEAGUE.

national game, the – In the 1850s, baseball was already widely known as America's "national game" (or "National Game," as it was sometimes written).

National League – One of two US major baseball leagues, consisting of 15 teams—five in each of three divisions: East, Central, and West. The National League (abbreviated NL) was founded in 1876, originally consisting of eight teams and no separate divisions. The league was administered by its own president and NL teams played AL teams only during the World Series each October (starting in 1903).[47] Since 1997, with the inception of interleague play, NL teams play up to 18 regular-season games against AL teams. After the 1999 season, the NL and AL merged into a single organization (Major League Baseball) presided over by the COMMISSIONER OF BASEBALL, and the league presidency became an honorary position. Since 2001, the honorary president of the NL has been Bill Giles, owner of the Philadelphia Phillies.

national pastime, the – In the 1850s, newspapers often referred to baseball as America's "national pastime." The term reflected the widespread love of baseball by Americans of all socio-economic levels, all ethnic backgrounds, all walks of life, in all parts of the country. The term eventually supplanted "THE NATIONAL GAME" as the favored sobriquet for baseball.

Negro leagues – Indisputably, the quality of major league baseball increased exponentially when Jackie Robinson broke the color barrier in 1947 and paved the way for African Americans and other people of color to play on major league teams in both leagues. But prior to 1947, players of color were barred from competing professionally with white players, and as a result, enterprising businessmen formed leagues where they could showcase their baseball talent.

Although generic "Negro leagues" existed as far back as 1885, the first official Negro league, the *Negro National*

---

[47] The AL came into existence in 1901.

86

League, was formed in 1920, consisting of teams from the Midwest. In 1937, the *Negro American League* was born, also composed of Midwestern teams. The season schedules in the Negro leagues varied in length, from 40 to 90 games. Negro league teams played numerous exhibition games against white major league teams, winning about sixty percent of them.

It's a reasonable assertion that many of the greatest ballplayers of the first half of the twentieth century were African Americans, and that fact was finally recognized in 1971 when pitching great Satchel Paige was elected to the Hall of Fame.

Between 1971 and 2006, 33 more Negro league players and one executive (the only female in the HOF, Effa Manley) were enshrined in the Hall.

Six Rules for Staying Young
1. Avoid fried meats which anger up the blood.
2. If your stomach disputes you, lie down and pacify it with cool thoughts.
3. Keep the juices flowing by jangling around gently as you move.
4. Go very light on the vices, such as carrying on in society—the social ramble ain't restful.
5. Avoid running at all times.
6. Don't look back. Something might be gaining on you.
—Hall of Fame Negro leagues and major league pitcher Satchel Paige

---

nibble around the edges – Refers to a pitcher aiming for the periphery of the strike zone, where the batter is more likely to either take the pitch, because it looks like a ball, or swing and miss. This strategy is normally wiser than aiming to throw pitches smack in the middle of the strike zone—which tends to result in base hits, long flies, home runs, and all sorts of mayhem for the pitcher's team.

nicknames – Baseball and nicknames go together like, well, baseball and hot dogs. Nicknames today aren't quite the big thing they used to be. Every ballplayer had a nickname years ago,[48] and in some cases they were so commonly used that few people even knew a player's given name. Take *Babe* Ruth, for example (given name, George), who was also known as the *Sultan of Swat* and the *Bambino*; or *Catfish* (Jim) Hunter; *Blue Moon* (John) Odom; *Stuffy* (George) Stirnweiss; *Vinegar Bend* (Wilmer) Mizell; and *Chipper* (Larry) Jones.

Many other ballplayers were well-known both for their given names and their descriptive nicknames (how many do you know?): *The Georgia Peach, The Commerce Comet, The Chairman of the Board, The Flying Dutchman, The Duke of Flatbush, The Man, The Old Perfessor, Mr. Cub, The Splendid Splinter, Say Hey, Pops, The Iron Horse, Killer, Joltin' Joe, The Tall Tactician, Sudden Sam, Rapid Robert, The Yankee Clipper, Teddy Ballgame, Yaz,* and *The Wizard of Oz.*[49]

---

[48] Not literally true, of course, but many, many did.
[49] Answers: Ty Cobb, Mickey Mantle, Whitey Ford, Honus Wagner, Duke Snider, Stan Musial, Casey Stengel, Ernie Banks, Ted Williams, Willie Mays, Willie Stargell, Lou Gehrig, Harmon Killebrew, Joe DiMaggio, Connie Mack, Sam McDowell, Bob

Of all the names and nicknames in baseball, I think my all-time favorite is the alliterative and euphonious name of a terrible St. Louis Browns pitcher of the late 1930s and early 1940s: Emil "Hill Billy" Bildilli. It just kind of trips off the tongue, doesn't it?

no-hitter – A game in which an individual starting pitcher, or a starting pitcher together with one or more relief pitchers, does not allow the opposing team a base hit the entire game.[50] No-hit games are rare—only occurring about once in 725 games. In major league history, dating back to the National Association in 1875, there have been only 300 no-hitters, of which 288 were by individual pitchers and 12 were "combined" no-hitters by two or more pitchers. Nolan Ryan, of the Angels, Astros, and Rangers, ranks first with seven no-hitters in his career; Sandy Koufax of the Dodgers is second with four.

Fun fact: Two pitchers in MLB history have pitched a no-hitter and *lost* the game. Ken Johnson of the Astros no-hit the Reds on April 23, 1964, but lost the game 1-0. Steve Barber of the Orioles combined with Stu Miller to no-hit the Tigers on April 30, 1967; Barber walked 10 batters and gave up two runs, losing the game 2-1.

nubber – A weakly hit ground ball to the infield that often results in a base hit for a fleet-footed batter. (Sometimes spelled "knubber.")

numbers on uniforms – For the first several decades of major league baseball, players wore nothing on their

---

Feller, Joe DiMaggio (again), Ted Williams (again), Carl Yastrzemski, and Ozzie Smith.
[50] An "entire game" can be as brief as five innings in length if it is shortened due to inclement weather (see OFFICIAL GAME).

uniforms to identify who they were—no names, no numbers. In 1916, the American League's Cleveland team was the first to wear numbers on the sleeves of their uniforms. Finally, in 1929 the same Cleveland club featured numbers on the backs of their jerseys, and by 1937 all major league teams had them.

OBA or OBP – Abbreviation for ON-BASE AVERAGE/PERCENTAGE.

objectives of the game – According to the official rules, baseball is a game played between two teams of nine players. One team plays defense (the team in the field) and the other plays offense (the team at bat). The teams alternate playing defense and offense for nine innings. The visiting team always bats first, in the top of each inning, and the home always bats last, in the bottom of each inning. "The winner of the game shall be that team which shall have scored . . . the greater number of runs at the conclusion of a regulation game."[51]

October Classic – Informal title for the WORLD SERIES.

official game – A normal, regulation major league baseball game is nine innings. However, if a game is shortened due to inclement weather (usually rain), it will count as "official" if at least five innings have been played (or four-and-a-half innings if the home team is leading after the visiting team has batted in the top of the fifth).

official scorer –The Office of the Commissioner appoints one individual to keep the official score of each game. One-fourth of the official MLB rule book is devoted to the role of the official scorer, who sits in the press box and keeps

---

[51] Rule 1.06 – "The Objectives of the Game," (Official Rules, 2017)

the official score of the game—all hits, walks, putouts, errors, etc. It is the official scorer who decides when a batter reaches base or a runner advances or scores because of a misplay by the defensive team and awards an error or errors accordingly. The official scorer determines therefore whether runs are earned or unearned. Following the game, the official scorer prepares a full report that is forwarded to the Office of the Commissioner.

on-base average/percentage – Abbreviated OBP or OBA. A calculated batting statistic (total hits + walks + HBP / total plate appearances). The range is .000 to 1.000. Normally, a player is said to have a high on-base percentage for the season if it is around .400, meaning he has reached base safely four out of ten times he has stepped into the batter's box.

[Baseball] is a haunted game in which every player is measured against the ghosts of all who have gone before. Most of all, it is about time and timelessness, speed and grace, failure and loss, imperishable hope—and coming home.

– Geoffrey C. Ward & Ken Burns,
authors & filmmakers

---

on-deck circle – When a player is up to bat, the next player in the batting order waits his turn in the on-deck circle near his team's dugout. Formally termed the "next batter's box," on-deck circles are five feet in diameter and located between the player's dugout and home plate.

OPS (a calculated statistic) – The sum of a player's (or team's) ON-BASE PERCENTAGE and SLUGGING PERCENTAGE. Normally, a player is said to have a high OPS if it is above .800. The OPS (an initialism pronounced *O-P-S*, not "opps") is the best easily calculated measure of an individual player's or team's offensive ability. There is a fairly strong, positive statistical correlation between a team's OPS and their winning percentage. The highest single-season OPS in MLB history for an individual player was Barry Bonds's 1.421 in 2004.[52]

OPS+ – A calculated statistic used to compare one player's OPS (see above) to the rest of the league, where 100 is average. An OPS+ of over 100 means the hitter's OPS is better than the league average, and an OPS+ less than 100 means the hitter's OPS is below the league average. The formula: (OPS / league OPS, adjusted for park factors) x 100. The highest OPS+ in major league history belongs to Barry Bonds at 268 in 2002, meaning his OPS production was a phenomenal 168% higher than the league average.[53] The AL record of 255 was set by Babe Ruth in 1920.

out/outs – Baseball is not played by the clock as most team sports are. It is played by innings, and innings are defined by outs. A regulation game is nine innings long. There are three outs in an inning for each team, thus six total outs per inning or 54 outs in a 9-inning game (or 51 outs if the home team, which always bats last, is ahead after the top of the ninth inning). The three most common ways batters

---

[52] How much did Bonds's alleged PED use influence this tremendously high number? We may never know.
[53] Again, how much of this can we attribute to PED use?

make outs are by GROUND OUTS, AIR OUTS,[54] and STRIKEOUTS.

outfield – The expansive area between the infield dirt and the outfield fence, between the foul lines, is the area known as the outfield. Left field is on your left as you look out from home plate, and right field is, um, on your right. Center field is—well, you get the picture. Usually, the speediest outfielder is in center field as he ranges to both left and right fields to back up those fielders. Typically, the right fielder has the strongest arm as he must often make the long throw to third base in an effort to put out baserunners. Of course, as in all of life, there are exceptions to these generalities.

pace-of-play rules – In 2017, the average length of major league games reached the all-time high of three hours and five minutes. Therefore, in 2018, new rules were adopted with a view to speeding up games (a little) in an effort to keep fans' interest from waning so that they keep the TV or the radio tuned in, and therefore help sponsors be better stewards of their advertising dollars. Plus (and this is less cynical) with baseball's popularity in America ever-gradually fading, speeding up games is meant to counter the frequently heard criticism that "baseball is boring."

So now, for example, each team is allowed a maximum of six visits to the pitcher's mound during a nine-inning game. These "visits" include the manager or coaches checking on the pitcher, or visits by catchers or infielders to plan strategy, confirm signals, or decide where they're going to

---

[54] *Air outs* is a fairly recent categorical term for outs made when balls hit into the air are caught by fielders. Normally, however, we say that a batter "flied out," or "lined out," or "popped out," or "fouled out," (that is, we don't say he "aired out").

eat after the game. Basically for any reason. In addition, batters are no longer allowed to step completely outside the batter's box between pitches; he must keep at least one foot in there at all times.[55] The amount of time between innings has been reduced slightly as well. One time-saving idea that baseball folks have bandied about has not been adopted yet: the pitch clock. Will it be adopted in 2019? We'll find out.

passed ball – A passed ball occurs when a pitch that the official scorer has judged to be catchable with ordinary effort—whether a BALL or a STRIKE—gets past the catcher and the baserunner(s) advance one or more bases. If no runner is on base, the pitcher is charged with a ball or strike. A passed ball is not counted as an ERROR, thus lowering a catcher's FIELDING PERCENTAGE, but any run that scores as a result of a passed ball is considered UNEARNED.

The major league record for passed balls in a single season in the MODERN ERA is 35, by Geno Petralli of the Texas Rangers, in 1987. Petralli also holds the record for most passed balls in one game—six, on Aug. 30, 1987 (tied with two others), and in one inning—four, on Aug. 22, 1987 (also tied with two others).

payoff pitch – The pitch thrown with a FULL COUNT.

PEDs – Performance enhancing drugs. It's a travesty that a term like this should even be considered in the context of the National Pastime. A number of superstar ballplayers allegedly used PEDs to bulk up their bodies and, correspondingly, their stats, such as home run totals. Jose

---

[55] This rule was actually adopted in 2015 but has been inconsistently enforced by umpires.

Canseco, Barry Bonds, Mark McGwire, Roger Clemens, Gary Sheffield, and others allegedly achieved near superhuman success on the diamond because of PEDs and, as a result, sadly, will likely never be enshrined in baseball's Hall of Fame.[56]

pennant/pennant race – Baseball has long awarded a pennant to the team finishing in first place in their league. The teams vying to win the championship are said to be in a pennant race. The winners of each league's pennant each season face each other in the WORLD SERIES.

perfect game – A game in which a starting pitcher does not allow a baserunner the entire game, and the pitcher's team does not allow a baserunner by committing an error. We say it was "27 batters up and 27 batters down" for the losing team. Perfect games are extremely rare—there have been but 23 in major league history.

Pesky's Pole – The FOUL POLE on the right field foul line at Boston's Fenway Park. So named for Johnny Pesky, Red Sox infielder in the 1940s and '50s who hit but six career homers at Fenway Park, nearly all of which cleared the fence at around 302 feet, close to the right field foul pole.

Interesting fact: Johnny Pesky was one of several ballplayer-patriots who gave up entire seasons of their baseball careers to serve in the U.S. military during WWII. In Pesky's case it was *three* full seasons (1943–45).

pickle – Another term for a RUNDOWN.

---

[56] For those interested in reading further on this unfortunate topic, I recommend *Game of Shadows*, by Mark Fainaru-Wada and Lance Williams (2006).

pickoff – With a runner on base—especially one who is taking a large LEAD—a pitcher will sometimes whirl and throw to the fielder covering the base in the hopes of putting out the runner. The fielder must tag the runner with the ball to make the out. When successful, this is called a pickoff. When unsuccessful, it is called a pickoff attempt.

pinch hitter – The manager of the offensive team may decide to replace a hitter with a substitute hitter, either because the hitter is a poor hitter (such as pitchers commonly are) or in certain strategic situations (such as bringing in a left-handed hitter to face a right-handed pitcher, or vice versa). Often, pinch hitters are used in late-inning situations when there is the potential for the tying or go-ahead run to score.

pinch runner – The manager of the offensive team may decide to replace a base runner with a substitute runner, either because the base runner is injured and unable to run, or because a faster runner is needed— especially in late-inning situations where the tying or go-ahead run is on base.

pitch – The pitcher's throw toward the CATCHER squatting behind HOME PLATE, with a player from the opposing team at bat. From the earliest days of organized baseball, the rules have specified that "the ball must be pitched, and not thrown, for the bat."[57] The most current rule defines a pitch as "a ball delivered to the batter by the pitcher," with

---

[57] Rule number 9 of the Knickerbocker Base Ball Club, September 23, 1845.

the additional comment that "all other deliveries of the ball by one player to another are thrown balls."[58]

pitch count – Also known as "number of pitches" (NP). Every pitch thrown by every pitcher in every game is kept track of by every team. Managers and pitching coaches closely monitor when their starting pitcher has reached a particular number of pitches—usually somewhere around 100—to help them decide if he might be getting tired and therefore need to be relieved.

pitcher – The player who pitches, not throws (see PITCH above) the ball from the pitcher's mound to the batter. On most MLB active rosters, 11 to 13 of the 25 players are pitchers, of whom typically five are starters—who take turns starting games throughout the season (see PITCHING ROTATION below)—and the rest are RELIEF PITCHERS who sit in the bullpen during games, awaiting the possible call from the pitching coach to enter the game. One pitcher on each team normally fills the role of the "CLOSER."[59] Do position players ever get called upon to pitch? On rare occasions that does occur, when all the relief pitchers have been used (e.g., in a long extra-inning game) or in a BLOWOUT, in which the manager decides to give his bullpen a rest and bring in a POSITION PLAYER—who perhaps pitched in college or high school—to get the final out (or two or three).

---

[58] *Official Rules of Major League Baseball* 2017, 148.
[59] Sometimes managers will use more than one relief pitcher in the role of closer—occasionally, for example, they'll use a left- *and* a right hander in that role; there is no rule that there must be only one.

pitcher of record – The pitcher who, at any given point in the game, stands to be either the winning or losing pitcher, which can change depending on the game situation. For example, a pitcher of record who is removed before the end of the game will remain the pitcher of record until the score becomes tied or a new lead is established, at which time a new pitcher of record is established.

pitcher's best friend – The DOUBLE PLAY.

pitcher's cardinal sin – Walking the opposing pitcher is a particular no-no for a pitcher, on the par of committing a major sin, for two reasons: (1) pitchers as a whole are notoriously weak hitters, so giving up a base on balls to a batter who is far more likely to strike out than rap a base hit is considered an egregious boo-boo; (2) since pitchers normally bat last in the lineup, walking him brings up the leadoff hitter, who is generally one of the ablest players in the opposing lineup in getting on base.

pitcher's mound – In the earliest days, the role of the pitcher was to toss the ball to the batter, who was expected to hit it, and that was how each play was initiated. The pitcher stood on the flat ground a mere 45 feet (or "fifteen paces") from home base and pitched underhand. The batter was king and the pitcher was as much a tool of the offense as the defense. But with the allurement of increased competition, pitchers began to experiment with increased velocity and throwing the ball in such a way as to make it drop and curve. In 1881, the distance from home plate to the pitching box (still no mound) was increased to 50 feet. In 1884, pitchers could begin to throw overhand if they wanted, which advantaged pitchers over batters. In an effort to provide greater balance between pitching and hitting, in 1893 the distance from home to the pitcher's box was increased to 60 feet 6 inches (what it is today), which was a boon to hitters. But to provide a bit of counterbalance, the pitcher's mound was introduced (finally). The mound could be as high as a home team wanted at first—the higher the mound, the greater the advantage to the pitcher. In 1903 the rules specified that the pitcher's plate should not exceed 15 inches above the base lines and home plate. Then in 1968, with a large strike zone and the 15-inch high pitcher's mound, run scoring reached an all-time low. Most fans want to see scoring, so in 1969 the height of the mound was reduced to 10 inches and the strike zone was reduced as well. Offensive production increased, and the 10-inch high mound exists to this day. By the way, the mound itself is 18 feet in diameter.

pitcher's park, a – An informal term for a ballpark that seems to favor pitchers over hitters—where runs scored are generally fewer, hitters' batting and slugging averages are generally lower, and pitchers' earned run averages tend to be lower than the league average. Contributing factors often include deeper distances to the outfield fence (thus harder to hit home runs), larger foul territories (thus more opportunities for fielders to catch foul balls), and favorable atmospheric conditions (such as prevailing winds that tend to blow *in* toward home plate).

pitcher's plate – The slab of rubber, 24 inches by 6 inches, located in the approximate center of the pitcher's mound. The pitcher must deliver his pitches with his pivot foot touching the pitcher's plate (also known as "the rubber"). The front edge of the rubber is 60 feet 6 inches from the rear point of home plate.

pitching rotation – Every major league team rotates through a set of starting pitchers to allow typically four days of rest between starts for each pitcher. This requires a set of five starters in the rotation. So, for example, if starter A pitches on June 20, starter B pitches on June 21, and so forth through starter E who pitches on June 24 (assuming no off-days in the team's schedule). Starter A would pitch again on June 25.

The five-man rotation today is the most common rotation; managers are free to modify it as necessary. Occasionally, because of an off day in the schedule (which is a day of rest for everyone), the manager may choose to skip the fifth pitcher's start and go with starter A instead as he is usually the team's top starting pitcher. Or, in such situations, the manager may elect to keep the rotation intact to give his top starter an additional day of rest.

Pitching is 75 percent of baseball.
– Connie Mack, Hall of Fame manager

*Good pitching will always stop good hitting
and vice-versa.*
– Casey Stengel, Hall of Fame manager

---

pitcher's rubber (or "the rubber") – See PITCHER'S PLATE.

pitchout – When a speedy baserunner with a reputation for stealing bases is on first base, sometimes the manager will signal for a pitchout if there are fewer than three balls in the COUNT. The pitcher throws the ball away from the batter, high and outside, to enable the catcher an unobstructed catch. If the runner is in fact attempting to steal during the pitchout, the catcher will be in a better position to attempt to throw out the runner.

plate appearance (PA) – Every time a batter steps up to the plate to face a pitcher, it is counted as a plate appearance. Not all plate appearances count as official AT-BATS, however. For example, a BASE ON BALLS, SACRIFICE HIT, SACRIFICE FLY, HIT BY PITCH, and CATCHER'S INTERFERENCE all count as plate appearances but not as official at-bats (for batting- or slugging average purposes).

platter – Another term for home base. Also an expression for ineffective pitching: "Smith served up a feast on a platter to the visiting team. They slugged three homers and scored seven runs in just two innings."

"Play!"– At the beginning of the game, after the defensive (home) team has taken their positions in the field and the first batter in the visiting-team lineup has stepped into the batter's box, the umpire-in-chief calls "Play!" (or "Play ball!"). The game has officially started and the ball is alive and in play.

playoffs – After the regular season, the winners of each of the six major-league divisions (three in each league) and two WILD CARD teams[60] vie for the AL and NL league championships. It begins with four teams in each league playing two best-of-five-game division series. The winners of each division series face each other in the best-of-seven-game league championship series. Finally, the winners of each league championship series—the PENNANT winners in

---

[60] The wild card teams are the two teams with the best won-lost records in each league after the division champs. The two wild card teams play a one-game playoff to determine which gets to advance to each league's division series.

each league—face each other for the title of "world champions" in the WORLD SERIES.

playing field – See DIMENSIONS OF THE PLAYING FIELD.

pop-up – A pop fly ball, hit not very deep—often staying in the infield. Sometimes the announcer calling the play-by-play will say, "He (the pitcher) popped him (the batter) up." A pop-up isn't an automatic out—a fielder has to catch it, of course—unless the pop-up is in the infield and there are runners on base with less than two outs. In that case, the umpire will invoke the INFIELD-FLY RULE.

position player – A player on the team who isn't a pitcher and who plays one of the eight other POSITIONS in the field.

positions – There are nine players in the starting lineup and nine position players in the field. They may not all be the same as the nine in the batting lineup, but we'll get to that.

Each player in the field is given a number based on his

position—a number that has nothing to do with the number on his uniform. Fielders are numbered 1 through 9. Nothing out of the ordinary there. I'll briefly explain the number given each position player and try to explain why he's given that number, which should make it easier to remember the scheme. We start with the pitcher.

1 = Pitcher. Why is the pitcher assigned number 1? Well, it's easy when you keep in mind who is the most

important player on the field.[61] Simple: It's the one who initiates everything that happens. And so the pitcher is assigned the number 1 on the scorecard.

2 = Catcher. It makes sense, doesn't it, that if each play begins with the pitcher, the fielder he is pitching the ball toward would be assigned number 2?

3 = First base. When a batter manages to hit a fair ball, he runs toward first base to begin what he hopes to be his counterclockwise trek around the bases. It makes perfect sense to assign the number 3 to the first base position.

4 = Second base. Once the batter makes it safely to first base, his next objective is second base. Thus that fielding position is assigned number 4.

5 = Third base. Here's where it can get a bit confusing if we logically deduce that the numbering continues with the next player on the infield past the second baseman, which of course would be the shortstop. It took me a while to remember this, but it makes perfect sense to assign number 5 to the third baseman if we keep in mind where the baserunner is headed once past second base: he's obviously hoping to get to third, so that position is number 5.

6 = Shortstop. A position created in the 1840s, it was "almost certainly . . . an adaptation of the cricket position

---

[61] Before anyone protests that all the players on the field are equally important—relax. Of course they're all important. When the ball is smashed on the ground toward the third baseman or on the fly deep to center field, at that moment, those fielders are the most important ones on the defensive team. In general, however, it is the pitcher—the one who initiates every play—who is the most important man on the field.

of long stop." At first, the shortstop (originally spelled *short stop*) was essentially a fourth outfielder, whose function was to assist in relays from the outfield. By the 1850s, the position was truly a fourth infielder.[62]

7 = Left fielder. We're going to number the outfielders from left to right. So guess what's next? . . .

8 = Center fielder. Yep! And finally . . .

9 = Right fielder. Simple as pie, right? Once you master this numbering system, SCOREKEEPING is a cinch (almost).

pull hitter – A right-handed batter who tends to "pull" the ball (i.e., hit balls to left field) or a left-handed batter who tends to hit balls to right field.

putout(s) – A fielding statistic. A fielder is credited with a putout when he catches a batted ball in the air (whether a fly ball, a line drive, a pop out, or a foul out), or catches a ball thrown to him by another fielder and he either steps on the base or tags the baserunner with the ball before the baserunner steps on or touches the base. A catcher is also credited with a putout when he catches and holds on to a third strike.

quality start – One of the newer pitching stats in baseball history, first introduced by a Toronto sportswriter in 1985. A starting pitcher is credited with a "quality start" when he pitches six or more innings and allows three or fewer earned runs—regardless of whether or not his team wins the game or is even leading when the starter finishes his day's work. It is assumed that a pitcher's team stands a reasonably good chance of winning a game if the opposing

---

[62] Dickson, 2009, 772.

team is held to three or fewer runs, at least until the late innings (innings 7–9) when relief pitchers should be available to hold onto a lead or save the game. The statistic has fallen under deserved scrutiny by many fans who argue that six innings pitched with three earned runs allowed is a 4.50 ERA—certainly nothing to brag about.

range – Refers basically to a fielder's ability to get to batted balls and field them successfully, including scooping up ground balls, snagging line drives, catching fly balls, and making accurate throws.

range factor (RF) – The range factor is a statistic designed to provide more information about a player's fielding contributions to his team than FIELDING PERCENTAGE alone provides. Whereas fielding percentage is a measure of a fielder's ability to make errorless plays—so that, basically, the higher the fielding percentage, the fewer the errors made—the range factor is a measure of how many successful fielding plays a player makes at his position per game (or per inning). To calculate a fielder's RF, sum his assists and putouts and divide by the number of his games played at that position.[63]

Here's an example: Left Fielder X, who handles 250 chances in 150 games one year and makes 3 errors has a fielding percentage of .988. His range factor is 1.65, meaning he has successfully handled an average of 1.65 chances per game (247 successful chances divided by 150 games played). Left Fielder Y, on the other hand, who handles 300 total chances in 150 games, but makes twice

---

[63] A more accurate RF formula divides the sum of assists and putouts at a particular position by nine and multiplies that number that by the innings played at that position. This yields a per-nine-innings statistic, similar to a pitcher's ERA.

as many errors (6), has a lower fielding percentage (.980), but his range factor is 1.96 (294 successful chances divided by 150 games played.

All other variables being even, who is the more effective outfielder? Probably Left Fielder Y, whose fielding percentage is lower but his range factor is higher. On average he made .31 more successful plays per game than Left Fielder X.

Is range factor a foolproof defensive statistic? No. Many baseball thinkers criticize RF because so many other variables can affect it, especially the pitching variables. But taken together with fielding percentage, it's a useful measure of a player's effectiveness as a fielder.

relief pitcher – Any pitcher who enters the game after the starting pitcher is removed from the game is called a relief pitcher. He is relieving the previous pitcher of his afternoon's or evening's duties. A reliever may pitch one inning, several innings, or just a portion of an inning—sometimes pitching to just one batter. Most pitchers on most MLB rosters have clearly defined roles as either starters or relievers, although a "long-relief" pitcher (one who is capable of effectively pitching two or more innings in relief) may occasionally be called upon to start a game on short notice if a regularly scheduled starter is suddenly hurt or becomes ill. Conversely, a regular starter may be sent to the bullpen to spend time as a relief pitcher for a time if he seems to be struggling to pitch effectively beyond the third or fourth inning.

retired – A batter is "retired" by making an out. When a pitcher faces three batters in an inning and each one makes an out, the pitcher is said to have "retired the side."

right down Broadway – A pitch thrown smack in the middle of the strike zone—typically resulting in a solid base hit for an even semi-alert batter.

Roberto Clemente Award – Considered by current Commissioner of Baseball Rob Manfred as "baseball's most prestigious award," the Roberto Clemente Award "is given annually to a player who demonstrates the values Hall of Famer Roberto Clemente displayed in his commitment to community and understanding the value of helping others. Each club nominates a player in September. The winner is selected from 30 nominees during the World Series. Originally the Commissioner's Award, the honor was named for Clemente in 1973."[64]

Rod Carew Award – Since 2016, the American League batting title has been named for seven-time AL batting champion Rod Carew, who played for the Twins and the Angels from 1967 to 1985, slashing 3,053 base hits. Carew posted a .328 career batting average,[65] and a single-season high of .388 in 1977. The first Rod Carew Award recipient was Jose Altuve of the Houston Astros, who batted .338 in 2016. Altuve also won the award in 2017 with a .346 average.

Rookie of the Year (ROY) award – As the title indicates, the player voted the most outstanding new (or rookie) player in each league is named the Rookie of the Year. Jackie Robinson of the Brooklyn Dodgers, who broke the color barrier in 1947, was the first award recipient. In the first two years of the award, only one rookie was so honored in MLB (in 1948 it was shortstop Alvin Dark of the

---

[64] Retrieved 9/5/17 fromhttp://m.mlb.com/awards/history-winners/?award_id=MLBRC&year=2014
[65] Currently thirty-fourth on the all-time leaders list.

Boston Braves). Starting in 1949, one outstanding rookie from each league has received the award. Today the ROY award is officially known as the Jackie Robinson Award. Each year, the Baseball Writers Association of America selects the top rookie from each league. The minimum required qualifications are 130 at-bats for a position player, 50 innings pitched for a pitcher, or 45 days on a major league roster.

room service – An expression with two different senses: (1) a fly ball (or line drive) hit straight to a fielder who hardly has to move to catch it; (2) a "fat" pitch (typically a fastball) right down the middle that is easy to hit.

rosin bag – A small cloth sack containing and covered with sticky rosin, kept behind the pitcher's mound, for the pitcher's use during the game—to dry his hands or enable a better grip on the baseball.

roster – Each major league team has an active roster of 25 players, from which managers select starting pitchers, batting lineups, pinch hitters and fielders, and relief pitchers for each game. However, those 25 players are part of the team's larger 40-man roster, which includes players on the 7- and 10-day disabled lists as well as additional players from their minor-league farm system who can be activated and "brought up" to the parent club as needed—usually to fill spots vacated by injured players on the DL. On September 1 each year, major league teams may activate and call up all players on their 40-man rosters.

rounders – A British sport using balls, bats, and "stations" (instead of bases) with pegs stuck in the ground. Rounders provided at least partial inspiration for the American game of baseball. Another British sport that contributed to baseball's genesis was TOWN BALL.

rubber, the – See PITCHER'S PLATE.

rubber game/match – The term used for the third and final game of a series in which each team has won one game.

rules of baseball – The first formal rules were written for the New York Knickerbocker Base Ball Club in 1845. There were twenty rules, the first of which was, "Members must strictly observe the time agreed upon for exercise [i.e., the game], and be punctual in their attendance." Today the Office of the Commissioner of Baseball publishes an updated copy of the official rules each year. The 2017 edition contained 162 pages.

run(s) – Some team sports score *points* (e.g., basketball) and some score *goals* (e.g., ice hockey and soccer). In baseball, players score *runs*, and the team with the most runs at the end of the game wins. A player scores a run when he makes it around the bases and touches home plate without being put out.

The record for the most runs scored by an individual player in one season in the MODERN ERA is 177, by Babe Ruth, in 1921. Rickey Henderson holds the record for most lifetime runs scored, with 2295.

The record for most runs scored by one team in a major league game in the modern era is 30, by the Texas Rangers against the Baltimore Orioles, on August 22, 2007.

run-and-hit play – A variant of the HIT-AND-RUN PLAY. A baserunner is given the green light to steal and the batter is allowed (by the base coach) to swing or not to swing at the ball. The difference between the run-and-hit play and the HIT-AND-RUN play is that in the latter, the batter is expected to swing at the pitch, to "protect" the runner.

run batted in (RBI)[66] – A batter is credited with an RBI when a baserunner scores as a result of the batter's BASE HIT,[67] BASE ON BALLS, SACRIFICE FLY, SACRIFICE BUNT, or hit by pitched ball. No RBI is credited when a runner scores on an ERROR, DOUBLE-PLAY, WILD PITCH, or BALK. The plural is *runs batted in* or RBIs (no apostrophe). Some fans and sportscasters use the casual term "ribbie(s)"—but not this writer.

rundown – A baserunner is caught in a rundown (also known as a "pickle") when he is midway between bases and apparently cannot make it safely to the base he is headed toward or the one he just left. Opposing fielders will, if correctly executing the play, throw the ball back and forth—in front of and behind the runner—once or twice or several times until one of them is able to tag the runner out *or* until the runner successfully eludes the tag and either advances to the next base or returns to the previous one. In the major leagues, a rundown most often ends in the runner being tagged out.

runs produced (RP) – One meaningful measure of a hitter's offensive value is this simply calculated statistic. The formula is *runs scored* plus *runs batted in* minus

---

[66] RBI is technically an initialism, like ERA and OPS. WHIP, on the other hand, is an acronym. In an initialism, each letter is pronounced individually; in an acronym, the letters are pronounced as a word.
[67] This includes when a batter drives himself in by hitting a home run.

home runs (or [R + RBI] – HR). I recently read an article that referred to this statistic as "points,"[68] advocating for its use as a good and simple way to conceptualize a player's offensive contribution, similar to how a hockey player accumulates points by adding his goals scored and assists.

So for example, a batter who scores 85 runs, drives in 90 more, and hits 30 homers has 145 runs produced, or points ([85+90]–30). The statistic becomes more meaningful when we divide RP by plate appearances to produce a stat similar to batting average or slugging average. For example, 145 RP divided by 530 plate appearances equals .273 (which means that the batter produced .273 runs per plate appearance).

sacrifice fly – With less than two outs and a baserunner on third base, a fly ball hit deep enough to the outfield (and caught by an outfielder) may enable the runner to TAG UP and score a run. When that occurs it is considered a sacrifice fly; no at-bat is charged to the batter, and he is awarded an RBI.

sacrifice hit – When a team has a baserunner on first or second base, or on first *and* second base, with less than two outs, a manager will sometimes have his batter attempt to advance the runner(s) one base by laying down a BUNT. The objective is for the defending team's first or third baseman (or pitcher or catcher) to field the ball and throw to first base to put out the batter. In so doing, the baserunner(s) will advance one base. Often (but by no means always) the batter is a relatively weak hitter (such as, in the National League, the pitcher). A successfully executed sacrifice hit

---

[68] Thomas 2018.

does not count as an at-bat for the batter, so does not affect his batting average.

save – In the most basic terms, a save is credited to a RELIEF PITCHER who enters a game with his team ahead and who finishes the game with his team still ahead. More specifically, there are three ways a pitcher can earn a save: (1) he enters the game after the fifth inning with his team ahead by any number of runs, pitches at least three full innings, and finishes the game with his team still ahead; (2) he enters the game with his team ahead by three or fewer runs and pitches at least one complete inning to finish the game with his team still ahead; (3) he enters the game with either one or two outs to go with his team ahead—with the tying or go-ahead run on base, at bat, or on deck—and finishes the game with his team still ahead.

save opportunity – An unofficial statistic for a relief appearance by a pitcher who enters the game in one of the three situations in which he could earn a SAVE. The statistic is useful in judging how effective a CLOSER is beyond a simple tallying of saves. For example, one closer earns 20 saves in 22 save opportunities (and therefore has only two BLOWN SAVES) for a 91% success rate. Another closer earns 20 saves in 28 opportunities (therefore has eight blown saves) for a 71% success rate. The first appears to be a considerably more effective closer.

save situation – Any of the three scenarios in which a RELIEF PITCHER who enters a ballgame can potentially earn a SAVE.

score (v.), or score a run – In baseball, the usual term for a team's putting up points on the scoreboard is the verb *to score*, or *score a run*, as opposed to *make a point*, or something similar. In basketball, a team scores points; in hockey and soccer a team scores goals. In baseball, teams score runs. If you want to sound like a savvy baseball fan, you will ask your friend, "How many runs did the Cubs score?", not "How many points did the Cubs make?"

Fun fact: In case you hadn't noticed, baseball is the only team sport in which scoring is not done directly with the ball. In basketball, points are scored when the *ball* goes through the hoop; in soccer and hockey, when the *ball* (or *puck*) goes into the net; in football, when the *ball* crosses the goal line or sails through the goal posts. In baseball, a run occurs when the *baserunner* touches home plate with the ball in play, wherever it is. Just a little trivia to throw out there at your next social gathering.

scorekeeping – Any fan can keep the score of a game in progress, which involves using a chart specially designed for the purpose. On the chart the scorekeeper lists the players for each team and uses a type of shorthand to  record each batter's actions as they occur (e.g., ground out, fly out, strikeout, base hit, home run, walk, reach on an error, RBI, etc.). After the game, a nerdy scorekeeper can fill in the summary stats on the portion of the score sheet that looks like a blank box score—usually on the right side for batters' stats and at the bottom for pitchers' stats. If you Google "baseball scorekeeping," you will find several variations on scorekeeping notations and styles. There isn't one "right" way to do it, although many notations are standard. For example, a groundout from shortstop to first is written 6-3 (or 63); a fly out to center is F-8 (or F8, or simply 8); a

113

strikeout is K (for a swinging strike three) or K written backwards for a called third strike (or K_c). If you score a game at the ballpark, you can purchase a scorecard there that includes a lot of great information about the teams and a blank two-page scoresheet.

scoring position – A base runner is in "scoring position" when he reaches second base because he can potentially score on any base hit, even a single, especially if he's a relatively fast runner. Obviously, a runner on third base is in scoring position as well as even the slowest-moving ballplayers should be able to score from third on a base hit.

screwball – A type of pitch that is thrown with an inward rotation of the arm (as opposed to the outward rotation used for the curveball). When thrown by a right-handed pitcher, the screwball will break down and in to a right-handed batter and down and away from a left-handed batter. It's vice versa for a left-handed pitcher: the ball breaks down and in to a left-handed batter and down and away from a right-handed batter. Hall-of-Famer Christy Mathewson popularized the pitch in the early 20th century, when it was called the "fadeaway." The pitch is difficult to master; therefore not many pitchers use it. Contrary to popular belief, throwing a screwball is not harder on a pitcher's arm than other types of pitches.

season, baseball – Baseball season spans roughly from mid-February, when spring training starts, through the last game of the World Series in late October or early November. The regular season schedule is 162 games—by far the longest in professional team sports[69]—and begins

---

[69] The next longest regular-season schedules are the National Basketball Association's and the National Hockey League's 82 games, followed by the National Football League's 16 games.

around April 1. The final regular season game is played at the tail end of September, and then the post-season playoffs begin. For many decades, major league teams played a 154-game schedule, and when the regular season ended, the next event was the World Series as there were no playoffs. The AL and NL pennant winners played each other in Series, which ended no later than mid-October.

seeing-eye single/base hit – A GROUNDER that finds its way past lunging or diving infielders into the outfield for a base hit.

senior circuit – The NATIONAL LEAGUE, the older of the two major leagues.

set position – One of two legal pitching positions (the other is the WINDUP). With runners on base, the pitcher usually pitches from the set (or stretch) position, in which he does not raise his arms above his head, which takes more time and therefore allows greater opportunity for a swift baserunner to STEAL a base.

seventh-inning stretch –The spectators at a ballgame are invited to stand and stretch after the top of the seventh inning. Traditionally, fans sing a song, such as "Take Me Out to the Ballgame" or "God Bless America." How the seventh-inning stretch originated is unclear, but the practice goes back at least to the year 1910. The best account of its origin was told by George Will, who said that the 300-pound U.S. President William Howard Taft struggled to his feet during the seventh inning of a ballgame one day in order to stretch his massive frame. All the spectators in the ballpark also stood in respect for the president. Thereafter, it became the tradition for fans to stand and stretch at that point in the game.[70] True story? I can't say, but it's as good as any other.

shift, the – A defensive move that is increasingly common in the STATCAST era is to realign fielders away from their typical positions in order to provide more coverage in certain parts of the field where PULL HITTERS tend to hit the ball. For example, Ted Williams was an extreme example of a left-handed pull hitter. Some teams began to shift their third baseman all the way over to second base and move their shortstop into shallow right field. Their left fielder would play roughly in center field and the center fielder would join the right fielder over in his territory. The goal of the shift is to reduce the likelihood of a base hit and increase the probability of fielding a batted ball and recording an out. Of course, truly talented hitters can sometimes foil the shift by hitting the ball to the opposite field, which has been left untended.

show, the – (Sometimes *show* is capitalized.) Informal synonym for the major leagues. Sometimes referred to as "the big show." Although the term has been in use since at least the first decade of the 20th century, it was popularized in the film classic *Bull Durham* (1988). In 1995, MLB introduced the slogan, "Welcome to the Show."

shutout – (n.) As a closed-compound, single-word expression, it is the term given to a game that ends in one team scoring no runs, usually applied to the pitcher (or pitchers) of the winning team: "Gibson pitched a *shutout* (noun) in St. Louis today." In verb form, it is written as two

---

[70] Will 1990, 172.

separate words: "The Cardinals' Bob Gibson *shut out* the Phillies this afternoon."

Silver Slugger™ Award – The full name is the Louisville Slugger® Silver Slugger™ Award.[71] Since 1980, managers and coaches from every major league team have voted in October on the previous season's top offensive producers at each fielding position. They evaluate players objectively based on their SLASH LINES as well as subjectively based on their impressions of the overall offensive contributions a player makes for his team. Managers and coaches may not vote for players on their own teams. Recipients receive a three-foot-tall silver-plated trophy with the names of all 18 winners engraved on it.

slash line – A relatively recent statistic—or more accurately, *grouping* of statistics—to provide a fuller picture of a player's offensive contributions than the traditional home runs, RBIs, and batting average. The slash line is a player's batting average, on-base percentage, and slugging average (in that order), depicted using slash marks to separate them. For example, if a player is batting .289, with an on-base percentage of .352 and a slugging average of .468, his slash line would be .289/.352/.468.

SLG – Abbreviation for SLUGGING PERCENTAGE (or slugging average, sometimes abbreviated SA).

slider – See TYPES OF PITCHES.

slugger – A hitter well-known for going yard, hitting the long ball, belting four-baggers, hammering homers, etc.

---

[71] http://www.slugger.com/en-us/silver-slugger-awards

slugfest – A game in which both teams score many runs on extra-base hits, particularly home runs.

slugging percentage (SLG) – A calculated batting statistic intended to measure a hitter's ability to, well, slug the ball. The formula is TOTAL BASES divided by AT-BATS. A slugging average of .500, which statistically represents one-half (or .500) of a total base each at-bat, is considered very good. Conceptually, with a .500 SLG, an everyday player who averages four at-bats per game will accumulate two total bases per game, which adds up to approximately 300 total bases over the course of a season. The league leader will usually top .600. In 2017, Giancarlo Stanton of the Miami Marlins led the National League with a .631 slugging percentage, and Mike Trout of the Los Angeles Angels led the American League, at .629. The all-time single-season slugging percentage record is .863, by Barry Bonds of the San Francisco Giants in 2001.[72] The all-time career slugging percentage leader is Babe Ruth, at .691.

"small ball" – See LITTLE BALL.

solo homerun (or "solo shot") – A HOME RUN hit with the bases empty, thus scoring one run. (From the Latin *sōlus*: alone.)

southpaw – A left-handed pitcher. No one seems to know exactly how the term came about, but a story as plausible as any is that a sports writer in Chicago in 1885 noticed that the ballpark was situated such that a left-handed pitcher's arm faced toward the south. Ever after, left-

---

[72] I am aware of the controversy over acknowledging this record because it requires that we accept as legitimate the inflated number of home runs Bonds hit in 2001. I choose not to make a judgment on that, but merely report the official MLB record.

handed pitchers were southpaws.[73] That's good enough for me!

"souvenir for a lucky fan" (or some variant of that phrase) – Either a home run ball or a foul ball that goes into the stands and is caught or retrieved by a spectator. Many times I've heard an announcer say something like, "There's a souvenir for a lucky fan." Major League Baseball invites fans to keep those balls with their compliments. This was not true in the early days of baseball, when one or two balls were expected to suffice for an entire game, thus necessitating that spectators toss balls back onto the field, and occasionally ballpark security had to scuffle with fans who tried to keep their prizes. Fans were first allowed to keep such balls as souvenirs in Boston in 1912,[74] but not all teams were ready to follow suit. That changed after the infamous beaning death of popular Cleveland Indians shortstop Ray Chapman by Yankees pitcher Carl Mays in the 1920 season, to this day the only death caused by an injury to a player during a major league game. It's easy to imagine a white ball turning gray from dirt and spit by the later innings, and then when the sun began to set in late afternoon—as it was on that fateful day in New York in 1920—it was often a challenge for batters to see pitches. It was reported that Chapman never tried to get out of the way of the pitch that killed him because he likely didn't see it in time. Afterwards, baseball commissioner Landis ordered teams to keep relatively clean and white balls in

---

[73] Eugene T. Maleska, *A Pleasure in Words* (New York: Simon and Schuster, 1981), 102.
[74] According to Dickson's *Baseball Dictionary*, p. 807; however, another source claims fans first kept "souvenir" balls in Chicago in 1916, and another said it was Pittsburgh in 1921. Take your pick.

play, and therefore fans could begin to keep balls that went into the stands.

But some fans aren't so "lucky" when a ball flies into the stands. One of the strangest things I personally ever witnessed at a big league ballpark occurred during one of my first MLB games, as a thirteen-year-old kid. I was at the Oakland Colosseum for an Athletics game, sitting with my friends in lower-deck box seats on the first base side of the diamond. The batter smacked a towering foul ball that looked as though it would land not far to our right. A boy from several rows down, probably nine or ten years old, took a bead on the arch of the ball, turned and started to scramble up the stairs as quickly as he could toward where he thought it would land. But he miscalculated slightly. The ball fell out of the sky like a smart bomb, nailed him smack on the top of his noggin—nearly knocking him off his feet—and bounced fifteen feet in the air. He grabbed his head with both hands, plopped down in the nearest aisle seat, and rocked back and forth. In a flash a worried stadium usher arrived to render succor. Eventually, the usher and a member of the boy's family walked (fortunately walked!) the visibly shaken lad up the steps to the first-aid station. That incident served as a good reminder to me, both as a player and a spectator: never take your eye off the ball.

spitball – An illegal pitch in which a pitcher lubricates the ball with spit or another slippery substance and which causes the ball to dip dramatically. It was outlawed in 1920, but in 1921 eight NL and nine AL pitchers were named as spitball pitchers and were allowed to use the spitball for the rest of their careers. However, *outlawing* the spitball and pitchers obediently refusing to *use* it are two different things, as attested by the notorious master of baseball doctoring, Gaylord Perry, in the 1960s and '70s, who was fond of using K-Y Jelly to make his pitches do unusual things. This led MLB to ban the spitball (again) in 1974, this time with harsher penalties for infractions. (Perry, by the way, is in the Hall of Fame.)

squeeze play (or suicide squeeze play) – Normally used with less than two out—but used very rarely—with a runner on third base the batter attempts to surprise the defense and lay down a perfect bunt simultaneous to the baserunner breaking for home. If all goes well, the runner eludes the tag and scores a run; when it does not go well—and it often does not, which is why it is rarely used—the runner is tagged out; he has essentially "committed suicide."

squibber – Same as a NUBBER.

Statcast – State-of-the-art tracking technology installed in all 30 MLB ballparks since 2015. Using two separate systems—a Trackman Doppler radar system and a high-tech Chyron Hego stereoscopic camera system, Statcast measures practically everything that moves on the playing field—from the speed and spin of pitches to the exit velocity of balls hit by batters; from the height and distance of home run balls to the speed of players running the bases, and much more. Statcast has added a whole new layer and dimension of precision measurements to a sport already steeped in STATISTICS. The data generated supposedly helps team management and coaches in the way they use players.

statistics – Baseball is well-known as a game of statistics (often shortened simply to "stats"). Everything is counted—every pitch and type of pitch thrown, every swing of every batter, every hit and type of hit, and so much more. There are dozens if not hundreds of statistics, carefully logged by official scorers and maintained by an official league statistician who is appointed by each League President.

Baseball fans love numbers. They like to swirl them around their mouths like Bordeaux wine.

– Author Pat Conroy

---

stay[ing] alive – When a batter is behind in the count, his goal is to keep from being struck out. If he has a "good eye," he might stay alive by taking balls or fouling off pitches.

steal – A baserunner who advances successfully from one base to the next (if no baserunner is occupying it) while the  pitcher is in his delivery is "stealing" the base. Typically, only a handful of major league players will steal more than 30 bases in a full season. The major league record for stolen bases by an individual in one season, set by Rickey Henderson of the Oakland Athletics in 1982, is 130. Lou Brock of the Cardinals holds the NL record, with 118 in 1974. Henderson also holds the career stolen base record with 1,406.

Someone may wonder if a batter can steal first base. The answer is no. A batter may reach base safely on a base hit, base on balls, hit-by-pitch, fielding error, catcher's interference, or a dropped third strike (That last one is probably as close as a batter can get to "stealing" first base, but it is not scored as a stolen base—it is considered a strikeout and either a wild pitch or passed ball.)

stolen base – See STEAL above.

straightaway – Sometimes we'll hear an announcer say that the defense is playing the batter to hit the ball straightaway, meaning that fielders are positioned in their normal positions and haven't shifted to the right or left. Thus, the centerfielder is positioned in dead-centerfield; the second baseman is positioned to the right of the bag in his normal position, and so forth. This is the default defensive alignment against batters who spray the ball to all fields. (See the diagram under the POSITIONS entry.) Fielders will typically shift right or left against PULL HITTERS, and occasionally that SHIFT will be dramatic.

streaks – Because major league baseball is a game of stats, facts, and trivia, individual and team streaks of various sorts have been tracked, admired, and debated by dyed-in-the wool fans from the earliest days. For example, here are three of the most notable and enduring streaks in major league history: (1) the longest hitting streak belongs to Joe DiMaggio of the New York Yankees, who in 1941 reached safely on a base hit in 56 consecutive games; (2) Orel Hershiser of the Los Angeles Dodgers owns the longest consecutive-scoreless-innings-pitched streak, with 59 in 1988; (3) Cal Ripken of the Baltimore Orioles played in 2,216 consecutive games from July 1982 to July 1996.

stretch, the – Synonym for the SET POSITION.

strike – A pitcher throws a strike when the batter a swings at a pitch and misses, or when the ball passes through the STRIKE ZONE and the batter TAKES it, or when the batter hits or bunts the ball FOUL.[75]

strikeout – (noun): Three STRIKES on a batter is an out on strikes—a strikeout. It is one of the THREE TRUE OUTCOMES in baseball.

striker – Originally, in the early-to-middle nineteenth century, the batter was called the striker. When pitchers hurled the ball toward the catcher behind home plate, there were three possible results: a fair strike, a foul strike, or a ball.

strike zone – According to the official rules, the strike zone is "that area over home plate the upper limit of which is a horizontal line at the midpoint between the top of the shoulders and the top of the uniform pants, the lower level is a line at the hollow beneath the kneecap. The Strike Zone shall be determined from the batter's stance as the batter is prepared to swing at a pitched ball."[76]

swinging for the fence – When a batter—particularly a slugger—takes a mighty swing at a pitch, whether he makes contact with the ball or not, it is said he is "swinging for the fence" (i.e., apparently trying to hit a home run). For most players, most of the time, this isn't a good idea. The batter tends to give his swing a pronounced uppercut, which often spells strikeout. Some of the greatest sluggers of all

---

[75] When there are two strikes in the count and the batter hits a foul ball, it is not counted as a strike. A batter can foul off pitches all day and "stay alive" at the plate. A bunted foul after two strikes does count as the third strike and the batter is retired.
[76] *Official Baseball Rules 2017*, 150.

time could get away with that. Babe Ruth was noted for his mighty uppercuts, which often did result in home runs. This is also true of a number of the game's all-time great sluggers, such as Mickey Mantle, Harmon Killebrew, Mark McGwire, Reggie Jackson, Willie Stargell, and others. They all struck out a lot, but when they made solid contact, all an opposing outfielder could do was turn and watch the ball sail over the fence.

switch-hitter – A batter who can hit from either side of the plate: left-handed (against right-handed pitchers), and right-handed (against left-handed pitchers). The theory—empirically proven—is that lefties generally hit right-handed pitching better than righties do, and vice versa. It is called "playing the percentages" when a manager stacks his lineup with right-handed hitters versus left-handed pitchers (and again, vice versa), or when he uses a pinch hitter who bats opposite the pitcher's throwing arm. This is why batters who can hit from both sides of the plate—switch hitters—are so valuable. Hall-of-Fame switch-hitters include Mickey Mantle, Eddie Murray, Tim Raines, and Chipper Jones. (Pete Rose, the all-time hits leader but ineligible for the HOF, was arguably the most famous switch-hitter, after Mantle.)

switch-pitcher – Is there such a thing? Yes, there is! (Although the phenomenon is much less common than a switch-hitting batter.) There have been a small handful of ambidextrous hurlers in major league history who could pitch with relatively equal ability right- or left-handed. Tony Mullane, who played from 1881 to 1894, winning 284 games, has his throwing arm listed officially in the Baseball Encyclopedia as "TB" ("Throws Both"). Currently, the LA Dodgers pitcher Pat Venditte pitches with either hand. As stated in his bio online: "Venditte typically throws with the hand needed to gain the platoon advantage" [meaning, he will usually throw left-handed versus left-handed batters and right-handed versus right-handed batters].[77]

tag – A verb that usually refers to a fielder putting out a baserunner by touching him with the ball, or with the ball in his gloved hand, or by touching a base while holding the ball. Note that a fielder may not tag a baserunner by throwing the ball at him and hitting him. If the baserunner knocks the ball out of the fielder's hand as he is tagging him, there is no putout; the runner is safe.

tag up – A baserunner must wait with his foot touching his base until after a fly ball or line drive is caught before trying to advance to the next base (typically from third to home on a SACRIFICE FLY, or from second to third on a deeply hit fly ball). If a baserunner fails to tag, the fielder may throw to the fielder covering the runner's base, thus putting him out; the fielder does not need to TAG the runner.

take a pitch – A batter "takes" a pitch when he watches the ball go past him without swinging—or when he CHECKS HIS SWING so that his bat does not cross the plane of home plate.

"Take Me Out to the Ball Game" (song) – Composed in 1908 by Albert Von Tilzer and Jack Norworth. The Tin Pan Alley song became associated with the SEVENTH-INNING STRETCH by the 1920s and quickly became major league baseball's unofficial theme song. It is believed that neither

---

[77] www.baseball-reference.com/players/v/vendipa01.shtml.

von Tilzer nor Norworth had ever seen a big league baseball game prior to composing the song.

Why do people sing "Take Me Out to the Ballgame" when they're already there?

– Relief pitcher Larry Andersen

Texas Leaguer/Texas League single – A term for a pop fly or soft line drive that lands in the shallow outfield beyond the reach of an infielder and in front of an outfielder. It's sometimes called a BLOOP SINGLE, or BLOOPER (also a *chinker, drooper, dunker, flare,* and several others). The origin of the term is disputed.

three-bagger – A TRIPLE (three-base hit).

throw, a – Here's how the official MLB rules describes a throw and how it's to be distinguished from a pitch: a throw is "the act of propelling the ball with the hand and arm to a given objective and is to be distinguished, always, from the PITCH."[78]

Tony Gwynn Award – Since 2016, the official title for award given the National League batting champion. The late Gwynn (1960-2014), elected to the Hall of Fame in 2007, was an eight-time NL batting champ with the San Diego Padres. He batted .338 lifetime, tied for eighteenth on the all-time list. DJ LeMahieu of the Rockies won the award in 2016, batting .348; Charlie Blackmon of the Rockies won it in 2017, batting .331.

---

[78] *Official Baseball Rules 2017,* 150.

tools of ignorance – Slang term for the equipment used by a catcher: the mitt, facemask, chest protector, and shin guards. Baseball writer Roger Angell attributes it to Washington Senators catcher Muddy Ruel (a lawyer in the off-season), who coined it in the 1920s.[79]

top of the inning – Each inning of a baseball game has two halves: the top half—or the "top of the inning"—when the visiting team bats, and the bottom half—or the "bottom of the inning"—when the home team bats.

total bases (TB) – The sum total of a batter's progression around the base paths resulting from base hits. A single counts as one base, a double is two, a triple is three, and a home run is four. For example, a player who hits a home run, a double, and two singles in a game has accumulated eight total bases. Shawn Green of the LA Dodgers set the record for most total bases in one game: 19, on May 23, 2002 (four home runs, one double, and one single). Babe Ruth established the record for most total bases in a season with 457 in 1921.

total chances – A fielding statistic. Each time a fielder makes a play on a ball, whether scooping up a grounder, throwing to a base, or catching a fly—or muffing a grounder, a throw, or a fly—it is considered to be a fielding chance. "Total chances," then, is the sum of a fielder's PUTOUTS, ASSISTS, and ERRORS. For example, a shortstop with three putouts, six assists, and one error in a game has tallied ten total chances. FIELDING AVERAGE is computed by dividing putouts plus assists by total chances. In the above

---

[79] Angell 1991, 204.

example, the shortstop's fielding average for the game is .900 (9 putouts and assists divided by 10 total chances).

town ball – A bat-and-ball sport played in America in the late eighteenth and early nineteenth centuries that evolved into the game of baseball (or *base ball*, as it was originally spelled) by the mid-nineteenth century.

triple – A three-base hit. In some ways, triples are the most difficult hit for major leaguers. Most batters will hit more singles, doubles, and home runs than triples over the course of a season. A player needs to be able to hit the ball into the gap in left- or right-center field that rolls to the wall, or into the corner in right field, and he needs to be fleet of foot. Lots of triples were a hallmark of baseball in the late nineteenth and early twentieth centuries. Sam Crawford, who played for Cincinnati and Detroit from 1899 to 1917, is the all-time triples leaders with 312. The all-time single-season record is 36, by Owen Wilson of the Pittsburgh Pirates, in 1912. The current *active* all-time triples leader is Jose Reyes of the New York Mets, with 128.

Many slow-footed batters play their entire careers hitting almost no triples. For example, Mark McGwire, who slugged 583 homers during a 16-year career, hit a grand total of six triples, four of which came in his rookie season.

Triple Crown – For most of major league baseball history, until very recently, three statistical categories provided the best collective snapshot of a hitter's offensive capabilities: HOME RUNS, RBIs, and BATTING AVERAGE. A player who leads his league in all three categories in the same season is said to have won the Triple Crown. That's always been a big deal, and it still is. And it is a rare feat. In major league history, the Triple Crown has been achieved only seventeen times, and only once in the past 50 years (by Miguel Cabrera of the Detroit Tigers, in 2012).

I said that "until recently" those big three hitting stats provided the best measure of a player's hitting ability—and, mind you, they are still useful and common. Broadcasters still show on the screen or announce a hitter's current batting average and home run and RBI totals. But today, other stats seem to tell a more complete story, such as the OPS (on-base average plus slugging average) or the SLASH LINE (batting average, on-base average, and slugging average), or even the WAR (Wins Above Replacement).

Pitching also has its Triple Crown: wins, earned run average, and strikeouts, although it is not an achievement officially recognized by the Elias Sports Bureau (as is the batting Triple Crown).

triple play – To make three outs in one play—an extremely rare fielding feat that can only happen with a minimum of two runners on base and no outs. For example, with runners on first and second, a batter hits a hard ground ball to the third baseman, who is playing close to the bag and steps on third base to force the runner coming from second for the first out and then quickly throws a bullet to the second baseman to force the runner coming from first for the second out; finally, the second baseman turns and fires a hot bullet to the first baseman to nail the batter charging up the base line for the third out. While easy to imagine, it's nearly impossible to execute as it requires a confluence of factors that almost never occur in baseball. Probably the most common triple play scenario (if "common" can be used in any sense to describe a triple play, which it can't) occurs with two (or more) runners on base (and no outs, of course), who take off running while the pitcher is in his windup. The batter hits a blazing line drive straight to, say, the second baseman for the first out, who either flips the ball to the shortstop covering second or himself steps on second for the second out (meaning, the runner who has left second base without TAGGING UP), who then fires the ball to the first baseman behind the runner charging toward second. An unassisted triple play—the rarest of all fielding feats—occurs when one fielder makes all three outs, as done by second baseman Bill Wambsganss of the Cleveland Indians against the Brooklyn Robins in the 1920 World Series.

true outcome/three true outcomes – A term coined for the baseball lexicon in August 2000. It refers to the three hitting outcomes that supposedly involve only the batter and the pitcher: the home run, the walk, and the strikeout. For example, no other fielder is involved in a home run (i.e., the pitcher delivers the ball, the batter hits it over the fence). There are no other variables coming to bear on the play. If a batter hits a ball that remains in play, any number of possible outcomes can occur: a base hit, an out, a foul ball, or an error. In those situations there isn't just one possible—therefore, one "true"—outcome. A strikeout is the same thing—a batter gets three strikes and he's out. In a walk, a batter gets four balls and he's on base. Aside from the catcher, who is responsible for calling pitches and catching the ball, no other fielder is involved in the play. It can be argued that there is no such thing as a "true outcome," as any number of possible things can occur every time the ball is pitched. But the concept has increasingly drawn the attention of sportswriters and fans in the past fifteen years because of the overall increase of home runs, walks, and strikeouts.

twin-killing – Another term for DOUBLE PLAY.

twinight doubleheader – A doubleheader in which one game is played in the afternoon and the second is played in the evening.

twirler – Slang term for the pitcher. Not heard much these days, but was fairly common in the early- to mid-twentieth century.

two-bagger –A DOUBLE (two-base hit).

If a woman has to choose between catching a fly ball and saving an infant's life, she will choose to save the infant's life without even considering if there are men on base.

– Humorist Dave Barry

---

types of pitches – Almost all professional starting pitchers have in their arsenal pitches from at least three categories: a fastball, a changeup, and a breaking ball.

Fastball – As the name implies, the fastball is a pitcher's fastest pitch. "Fast," of course, is a relative term. Some pitchers' fastballs are clocked in the 80-90 mph range, while others—the "power pitchers"—throw in the 90-100 mph range. A small handful of power pitchers—usually short-relievers—can reach upwards of 105 mph with their fastballs. Types of fastball pitches include the two-seam fastball, the four-seam fastball, the cutter, the sinker, and the split-finger fastball (or splitter).

Changeup – A pitch that's all about deception: the pitcher's motion and arm speed are identical to that used with a fastball, but because of the way the pitcher holds the ball, it is much slower than the typical fastball, which causes hitters to swing too early.

Breaking ball – A pitch that drops—or breaks—down and away from (or toward) the batter. The most common breaking pitches are the CURVEBALL, slider, SCREWBALL, and forkball.

Other, less common, pitches are the KNUCKLEBALL, and the eephus—two variants of slower pitches. The latter is an absurdly slow, high-arcing pitch that is intended to mess with a hitter's timing. The eephus is almost never seen, but when it is, it's comical.

umpire – While most other team sports have referees, baseball has umpires. The first set of baseball rules, adopted by the New York Knickerbocker club in 1845, called for "an Umpire, who shall keep the game in a book provided for that purpose, and note all violations of the By-Laws and Rules during the [game]." The umpire was to settle "disputes and differences relative to the game," and there was no appealing his decisions.[80]

In the early days of major league baseball, only one umpire officiated a game. In modern times, the rules specify that the league president shall appoint one or more umpires for each game. The umpires represent Major League Baseball and have the authority to enforce all the rules. Four umpires officiate at regular season games[81]—one positioned at each base, with the plate umpire, positioned

---

[80] Peverelly 1866/2005, 12.
[81] Six umpires normally officiate at the All-Star Game in July and in World Series games. The two additional umpires are positioned on the left- and right-field foul lines, midway between third- and first base respectively and the outfield fence.

behind the catcher, serving as umpire-in-chief. The umpire-in-chief is ultimately in charge of the playing of the game.

Where did the word "umpire" come from? When two teams compete, they do so as equals. They need a third party who is not an equal to serve as referee and oversee the game, make judgments, and arbitrate potentially disputable calls. He (or she) must not be on the same level as the players— not on a par with them. In ancient Latin he was a *non-par*; in Old French he was a *noumpere*. By the early seventeenth century, the *n* had fallen away and this referee became (voila!) *an umpire.*[82]

Uncle Charlie – A nickname for the CURVEBALL.

unearned run – As far as a game's OFFICIAL SCORER is concerned, every run scored is either "earned" or "unearned." In simplistic terms, a run is "earned" if it was scored as the result of error-free play by the defense. If, however, the official scorer deems that a run was scored as a result of a fielding error, it is considered "unearned." In fact, any and all runs that score in an inning after what should have been the third out, if the defense had played errorless ball, are considered unearned. Again, this is a call made by the official scorer.

uniform – All major league teams have at least two versions of their official costume, or uniform: one worn at home (usually predominantly white) and one worn on the road (usually predominantly gray). The first "modern" baseball uniforms, which included knickerbocker-style pants and

---

[82] Mish 1991, 482-83.

long stockings, were worn by ballplayers from 1869 onward.

walk – Another name for a BASE ON BALLS. Although batters who receive a base on balls are granted a free pass to first base—thus removing the need to sprint up the baseline, resulting in the informal term *walk*—very few players literally walk the entire distance from home to first. Most jog; a few sprint. (Pete Rose was a classic example of a player who sprinted full speed to first on a base on balls, which was partly responsible for his nickname "Charlie Hustle."[83])

walk-off – Refers to the game-winning hit in the home team's last at bat. For example, the home team is behind 5–4 in the bottom of the ninth, with runners on first and third. Jones strokes a double into the gap in right-centerfield, scoring both runners. The home team wins the game 6–5 on Jones's walk-off double. The term is also used when a bases loaded walk forces in the winning run (i.e., a "walk-off walk").

wall – Another word for the FENCE (or outfield fence).

WAR – An acronym for one of the newest baseball statistics, one that serious baseball fans, sports writers and baseball websites now bandy about with regular frequency: **W**ins **A**bove **R**eplacement. The formula is complex, but its intent is to provide one magic number that somehow represents The Value of a ballplayer—sort of like reducing the meaning of the universe to one pithy phrase. The WAR

---

[83] Pete Rose, aka "Charlie Hustle," baseball's all-time hits leader with 4,256 base hits, would easily be in the Hall of Fame today had he not been banned from baseball for life in 1989 by Commissioner A. Bartlett Giamatti for betting on his own team.

statistic is the number of wins a ballplayer is worth above that of a typical replacement player at his position, taking into account both his offensive *and* defensive stats. So, for example, the player with the all-time highest WAR in a single season was Babe Ruth in 1923, at 14.1. By comparison, the major league WAR leader in 2017 was Jose Altuve of the Astros, at 8.3. It's an interesting stat, but the complexity of its formula means that most fans (this author included) can't calculate it for a player.

warning track – The dirt band[84] 10–15 feet wide that encircles the playing field between the grass and the fence. Outfielders who are looking up while chasing a fly ball or foul ball over their heads will know they are about to crash into the wall when they step onto the warning track. Warning tracks first appeared in the mid-twentieth century, beginning with Wrigley Field in Chicago. In 1947, Pete Reiser of the Brooklyn Dodgers was seriously injured crashing into the wall at Ebbets Field. The following season, the Dodgers covered the outfield wall with foam rubber. Soon all team owners decided it might be a good idea to protect their human capital and so installed warning tracks in every ballpark.

waste (a pitch) – To intentionally throw a pitch outside the STRIKE ZONE, expecting the batter to take it for a ball, but hoping for a swing and a miss. Usually thrown in situations where the pitcher is AHEAD IN THE COUNT.

WHIP – A calculated pitching statistic: Walks plus hits allowed, divided by innings pitched. (Pronounced *whip*, a true acronym.) It is a measure of a pitcher's ability to keep opposing players off base, which is the main function of the

---

[84] The warning track may also consist of cinders or rubber.

pitcher. The lower the WHIP the better. The WHIP statistic is the best easily calculated measure of an individual's or team's pitching effectiveness.[85] The WHIP came into prominent use in the 1980s and '90s.

whitewash – A SHUTOUT.

wild card team – At the end of each season, the teams finishing first in each of the three divisions in both the American and National Leagues automatically earn spots in their respective league's playoff series. In addition, the two teams with the next-best won-lost records in each league face each other in a one-game playoff to determine which of the two will go to the postseason as the wild card team. This creates a PLAYOFF system with four teams in each league vying ultimately for the league pennant.

wild pitch – A wild pitch is charged against the pitcher when a pitch outside the strike zone that the official scorer deems could not have been caught by the catcher allows the baserunner(s) to advance one or more bases. Any run that scores as a result of a wild pitch is charged as an EARNED RUN.

win(s) – Naturally, the team that scores more runs than their opponent in a given game wins the game. In addition, one pitcher from the victorious team is given official credit with the win; he is the winning pitcher (*WP* in the box score).

The benchmark of an outstanding season by a pitcher is—and has been for many decades—twenty wins. The last

---

[85] My own statistical research years ago determined that the WHIP is consistently the most closely correlated pitching statistic to winning percentage—more so even than ERA.

pitcher to win as many as 30 games in a season was Denny McLain of the Detroit Tigers, in 1968 (his final 31-6). Today, few pitchers get enough starts or pitch enough innings to win even 20 games, let alone 30.

The pitcher with the most career wins in major league history is Cy Young, who pitched from 1890 to 1911, notching 511 wins. The second-winningest pitcher is Walter Johnson of the Washington Senators (1907– 1927) with 417 wins. As of this writing, the active pitcher with the most career victories is Bartolo Colon, with 247 wins over a span of 21 seasons.

(See also WINS AND LOSSES below.)

windup – The windup position is one of two legal pitching positions (the other being the SET POSITION), in which the pitcher raises both hands above his head before delivering the pitch toward the batter. In the early days of baseball pitchers often made elaborate windup motions before each pitch, sometimes swinging both arms simultaneously in one or two windmills before starting his kick and releasing the ball toward the batter. You won't see such exaggerated windup motions today, but each pitcher adopts his own unique style. When bases are empty, a pitcher will typically use his full windup. When men are on base, he will usually pitch from the SET POSITION (sometimes referred to as the STRETCH).

winning percentage (a calculated team or pitching statistic) – A team and an individual pitcher has a winning percentage, the formula for which is wins/(wins + losses), and is always rounded to the third decimal. For example, the winning percentage for a team with a WON-LOST RECORD of 56–30 would be 56/(56+30) [or 56 divided by

86] = .651. The winning percentage for a pitcher with a won-lost record of 12–11 would be 12 divided by (12+11) [or 12 divided by 23] = .522.

wins and losses – Each win and loss a team incurs is credited to a pitcher. A starting pitcher is awarded a win if he pitches a complete game that his team wins, *or* if he pitches a minimum of five innings and his team is leading when he leaves the game and his team remains in the lead until the end of the game. If either of these situations does not occur and his team wins, a pitcher other than the starting pitcher is awarded the win. Any PITCHER OF RECORD whose team falls behind while he is pitching and remains behind until the end of the game is credited with the loss.

women's professional baseball – The All-American Girls Professional Baseball League, organized by business magnate Phillip Wrigley to help fill the void in the U.S. sporting scene created by World War II, existed from 1943 to 1954. In their first year, four teams played approximately 80 games each. Pitches were delivered underhand from 40 feet, the ball had the diameter of a softball, players wore skirts, and the distances between bases were short. Playing field dimensions were a lot like those of today's Little League fields. In time, the number of games increased, the diameter of the ball decreased, pitches were delivered overhand, and field dimensions and distances between bases were increased.

won-lost record (or win-loss record) – Both teams and pitchers have won-lost records. For the team, it's what appears in the daily league standings, always followed at least by the team's WINNING PERCENTAGE and GAMES BEHIND the division leader. A team's pitchers' won-lost records over the course of a season will of course add up to the team's overall won-lost record.

wooden glove (also IRON GLOVE) – If a ballplayer is a subpar fielder, a bit awkward and prone to committing errors—particularly, dropping or bobbling the baseball—it's said he has a "wooden glove." Few ballplayers of major league caliber are that consistently poor at fielding, so the label is sometimes applied to poor fielders *relative* to others in the league at their position.

World Series (WS) – The annual best-of-seven series of games played between the American and National League champions. The World Series takes place in October,[86] after the respective AL and NL division championship series. As a best-of-seven series, the winner is the first team to win four games, which earns them the title of baseball's "world champions." Some critics charge that the *world* in World Series is overreaching as it involves only U.S. teams (except for the Toronto Blue Jays, the only non-U.S. major league team. Several countries have professional baseball leagues, such as Japan, Mexico, Cuba, The Dominican Republic, and South Korea, and it is sometimes argued that a true "world series" should include them. But then, teams from those countries would have to belong to Major League Baseball, and one can imagine the logistical nightmare of adding, say, five to fifteen international teams to MLB and creating an interesting,

---

[86] Therefore its common nickname, "October Classic." Sometimes it is called the "Fall Classic."

equitable, plausible schedule that includes all teams. It's not likely to happen in my lifetime anyway.

The first World Series was played in 1903 between the Boston Americans and the Pittsburg Pirates.[87] At the time it was called the "World's Championship Series." It was a best-of-nine-games series that Boston won 5 games to 3. No World Series was played the next year, in 1904, but it resumed in 1905 and the Series has been played every year since.

The New York Yankees have the most World Series appearances and championships in major league history (40 and 27 respectively). The New York/San Francisco Giants are second in WS appearances (20) and the St. Louis Cardinals are second in WS championships (11).

The gods decree a heavyweight match only once in a while and a national election every four years, but there is a World Series with every revolution of the earth around the sun. And in between, what varied pleasure long drawn out!

– Jacques Barzun, in
"God's Country and Mine"

---

[87] Note: the Boston team was nicknamed simply the "Americans" in 1903—"Red Sox" came several years later. Contrary to popular legend, there is no evidence that they were known as the "Pilgrims" in 1903, although that nickname is commonly listed in baseball almanacs and encyclopedias. Pittsburg was spelled without the *h* in 1903.

worm burner – A sharply hit ground ball. (See also DAISY CUTTER and GRASS CUTTER.)

yard – Slang for baseball field or ballpark. (See also GO YARD.)

People will forever say to me, "I love to hear your voice because it reminds me of when I heard it a long time ago. It reminds me of summer nights in the backyard with my dad."

– Vin Scully, legendary Brooklyn and Los Angeles Dodgers broadcaster

Game Called

By Grantland Rice ©
Published: 1956
[Appeared in *The Fireside Book of Baseball*]

Game Called. Across the field of play
the dusk has come, the hour is late.
The fight is done and lost or won,
the player files out through the gate.
The tumult dies, the cheer is hushed,
the stands are bare, the park is still.
But through the night there shines the light,
home beyond the silent ill.

Game Called. Where in the golden light
the bugle rolled the reveille.
The shadows creep where night falls deep,
and taps has called the end of play.
The game is done, the score is in,
the final cheer and jeer have passed.
But in the night, beyond the fight,
the player finds his rest at last.

Game Called. Upon the field of life
the darkness gathers far and wide,
the dream is done, the score is spun
that stands forever in the guide.
Nor victory, nor yet defeat
is chalked against the player's name.
But down the roll, the final scroll,
shows only how he played the game.

(Written on August 16, 1948, after Rice learned of the death of
Babe Ruth. Incidentally, Rice coined the phrase that is now cliché,
"It's not whether you win or lose, it's how you play the game.")

Bibliography

Angell, Roger. 1991. *Once More Around the Park: A Baseball Reader*. New York: Ballantine Books.

n.d. *Baseball Almanac*. Accessed 2017. www.baseball-almanac.com.

Baseball, Mr. 2001. "The Doubleday Myth." *Mr. Baseball*. Accessed July 23, 2001. www.mrbaseball.com/history/doubleday.htm.

Brosnan, Jim. 1962. *Pennant Race: The Classic Game-By-Game Account of a Championship Season, 1961*. New York: Harper.

Bucek, Jeanine, ed. 1996. *The Baseball Encyclopedia*. Tenth. New York: Macmillan.

Burgos Jr., Adrian. 1997. "Playing Ball in a Black and White 'Field of Dreams': Afro-Caribbean Ballplayers in the Negro Leagues, 1910-1950." *The Journal of Negro History* (Association for the Study of African American Life and History) 82 (1): 67-104. Accessed November 4, 2017. http://www.jstor.org/stable/2717497.

Commissioner of Baseball. 2017. *2017 Official Rules of Major League Baseball*. 2017. Chicago, IL: Triumph Books LLC.

Dickson, Paul. 2008. *Baseball's Greatest Quotations*. Revised. New York: Harper Collins.

—. 2009. *The Dickson Baseball Dictionary*. Third. New York: W.W. Norton & Company.

Forsyth, Mark. 2011. *The Etymologicon: A Circular Stroll Through the Hidden Connections of the English Language.* New York: Berkley Books.

Froke, Paula, Anna Jo Bratton, and Oskar Garcia, . 2017. *The Associated Press Stylebook and Briefing on Media Law 2017.* 52nd. New York: Basic Books.

Heaphy, Leslie A. 2007. "More than a Man's Game: Pennsylvania's Women Play Ball." *Pennsylvania Legacies* (The Historical Society of Pennsylvania) 22-25, 27. Accessed September 2017.

James, Bill. 1982. *The Bill James Baseball Abstract 1982.* New York: Ballantine Books.

—. 1985. *The Bill James Historical Baseball Abstract.* New York: Villard Books.

—. 2001. *The New Bill James Historical Baseball Abstract.* New York: The Free Press.

Jazayerli, Rany. 2000. "Doctoring the Numbers: The Doctor Is . . . Gone." *Baseball Prospectus.* August 15. Accessed June 19, 2018. www.baseballprospectus.com/news/article/724/doc toring-the-numbers-the-doctor-is-gone/.

Jensen, Don. 2005. *The Timeline of Baseball.* New York: Palgrave Macmillan.

Kiner, Ralph, and Danny Peary. 2004. *Baseball Forever: Reflections on 60 Years in the Game.* Chicago: Triumph Books.

Leerhsen, Charles. 2015. *Ty Cobb: A Terrible Beauty.* New York: Simon & Schuster.

Mazer, Bill, and Stan and Shirley Fischler. 1990. *Bill Mazer's Amazin' Baseball Book: 150 Years of Baseball Tales and Trivia.* New York: Zebra Books.

Mish, Frederick C., ed. 1991. *The Merriam Webster New Book of Word Histories.* Springfield, MA: Merriam-Webster Inc.

Morse, Jacob. 1984. *Sphere and Ash: History of Baseball (1888).* Reissue of 1888 edition. Columbia, SC: Camden House.

n.d. *National Baseball Hall of Fame.* Accessed March 2018. https://baseballhall.org/.

Nemec, David. 2006. *The Official Rules of Baseball Illustrated.* Guilford, CT: The Lyons Press.

Nemec, David, Stephen Hanks, and Dick Johnson. 1992. *20th Century Baseball Chronicle.* Montreal: Tormont Publications.

Newman, Edwin. 1992. *Edwin Newman on Language.* New York: Galahad Books.

Norman, Jim. 2018. "Football Still Americans' Favorite Sport to Watch." *Gallup, Inc.* Gallup World Headquarters. January 4. Accessed April 30, 2018. http://news.gallup.com/poll/224864/football-americans-favorite-sport-watch.aspx?

Peverelly, Charles. 1866; 2005. *Peverelly's National Game.* Edited by John Freyer and Mark Rucker. Charleston, SC: Arcadia Publishing.

Pinker, Steven. 2011. *Words and Rules: The Ingredients of Language.* New York: Harper Perennial.

Reavy, Kevin, and Ryan Spaeder. 2016. *Incredible Baseball Stats: The Coolest, Strangest Stats and Facts in Baseball History*. New York: Sports Publishing.

Samantha. 2016. *When and Why the Pitcher's Mound Was Introduced to Baseball*. March 21. Accessed June 1, 2018. www.todayifoundout.com/index.php/author/samantha/.

Shulman, David. 1996. "On the Early Use of Fan in Baseball." *American Speech* (Duke University Press) 71 (3): 328-331. Accessed April 11, 2018.

Siwoff, Seymour, ed. 2018. *Elias Book of Baseball Records*. 2018. New York: Elias Sports Bureau.

Stewart, Wayne, ed. 2007. *The Gigantic Book of Baseball Quotations*. New York: Skyhorse Publishing.

Thomas, G. Scott. 2018. "The Producers." *Street & Smith's 2018 Baseball Yearbook*, February: 22-25.

Thorn, John. 1998. *Treasures of the Baseball Hall of Fame*. New York: Villard.

Verducci, Tom. 2017. "Real Men Have Curves." *Sports Illustrated*, May 29: 36-43.

Will, George F. 1990. *Men at Work: The Craft of Baseball*. New York: Harper Perennial.

Zinsser, William. 2003. *Spring Training*. Pittsburgh, PA: University of Pittsburgh Press.

[Baseball] breaks your heart. It is designed to break your heart. The game begins in the spring, when everything else begins again, and it blossoms in the summer, filling the afternoons and evenings, and then as soon as the chill rains come, it stops and leaves you to face the fall alone.

– A. Bartlett Giamatti, "The Green Fields of the Mind," November 1977.

Acknowledgements

Writing a book of almost any length is a major project. From the idea stage, to the initial outlining, to the gathering of materials, to the writing and rewriting and revising (and revising and revising)—all of it is a lengthy process for which there are no substitutes. I'm grateful for my wife, Glenda, who patiently listened to my ideas and reports of my progress over the months of writing, and who used her eagle eye to proofread the manuscript. If there are still errors or typos, the responsibility is solely mine.

I'm grateful for my son, Evan—who loves baseball (and the Dodgers) as much as I do—and who provided valuable feedback early in the revision process that led me to change my original title and cover artwork.

My daughter, Lindsey, happily adopted her dad's and big brother's enjoyment of baseball, appreciation of baseball cards, and love for the Dodgers. She still roots faithfully for the Boys in Blue.

I'm grateful for my brother Ken, who first planted the seeds that led to my love of baseball, the Minnesota Twins, and Harmon Killebrew.

I'm thankful for my cousin Vaughn, who taught me how to keep score when I was just a kid.

Michael Cieslinski, designer and publisher of the best baseball board game ever, gave me express permission to include the logo of that game, Dynasty League Baseball, in the entry on baseball board games. Thank you, Mike.

Notes